Leading with Your Heart

Leading with Your Heart:
Diversity and *Ganas* for Inspired Inclusion

Cari M. Dominguez and Jude Sotherlund

Society for Human Resource Management
Alexandria, Virginia
www.shrm.org

Society for Human Resource Management
Haidian District Beijing, China
www.shrm.org/cn

Strategic Human Resource Management India
Mumbai, India
www.shrmindia.org

The Society for Human Resource Management (SHRM) is the world's largest association devoted to human resource management. Representing more than 250,000 members in over 140 countries, the Society serves the needs of HR professionals and advances the interests of the HR profession. Founded in 1948, SHRM has more than 575 affiliated chapters within the United States and subsidiary offices in China and India. Visit SHRM Online at www.shrm.org.

Interior and Cover Design: Blair Wright

Library of Congress Cataloging-in-Publication Data

Dominguez, Cari M., 1949-
Leading with your heart : diversity and ganas for inspired inclusion / Cari M. Dominguez, Jude Sotherlund.
     p. cm.
  Includes bibliographical references and index.
  ISBN 978-1-58644-153-1
  1. Diversity in the workplace. 2. Leadership. 3. Personnel management. I. Sotherlund, Jude. II. Society for Human Resource Management (U.S.) III. Title.
  HF5549.5.M5D66 2009
  658.4'092--dc22
                              2009040392

10 9 8 7 6 5 4 3 2   10-0367

Contents

Acknowledgments

This book is the product of many years of conversations we have had in our quest to foster fairness in the workplace while furthering the goals of diversity and inclusion. Having worked closely together 20 years ago in the creation and implementation of the U.S. Department of Labor's Glass Ceiling Initiative and having remained engaged in this quest ever since through various high-profile appointments and assignments, we concluded that there were lessons learned and a message to be shared, a message rather simple in concept, yet difficult in its application.

It is our hope that in this book you will find what we believe is the essence of what drives results and moves us closer to the final destination of a truly diverse and inclusive workplace: leading with the convictions of your heart. It is the coupling of a keen business sense and functional expertise with the sincerest qualities of the heart — integrity, empathy, and compassion — that will lead to the desired results. For some, it might mean going it alone for a while, and we applaud you. For those whose efforts have been more a series of stops and starts, we encourage you to glean the best of each practice, refine and retool.

We greatly appreciated the support and assistance of all who made this book possible: the dozens and dozens of individuals whose work experiences were shared with us; the companies and leaders who provided examples of heartfelt leadership, and the organizations whose research and findings served to further inform our work.

We are particularly indebted to SHRM for enabling this book to come to fruition. To Christopher Anzalone, book publishing manager, who was with us every step of the way, providing invaluable guidance and counsel; to the SHRM readers: Lewis J. Benavides, Texas Women's University; K. Joy Chin, Jackson Lewis LLP; and Shaunice Hawkins, Evolutions Consulting, who offered feedback and suggestions that served to enhance the quality of the manuscript; to Gary Rubin, chief publishing and e-media officer and group publisher for SHRM, who, along with members of the editorial board, buoyed our spirits with their vote of confidence for this effort; and to all others who took part in the publishing, marketing, and distribution of this book, we are forever grateful.

Finally, we want to thank each other. Just as it did over 20 years ago, our collaboration served to strengthen our friendship and mutual professional respect. Two heads were clearly better than one, as we complemented each other in style, focus, and points of view. To our families — Bert, Jason, and Adam Dominguez and Dana, Emily, and Nicholas Sotherlund — thank you for your encouragement, patience, and selfless support. Any undertaking of this nature takes precious time. We can only hope that this investment of time and effort will inspire many, many others to lead with their hearts, leaving behind attitudinal barriers and assumptions of the past. Our new generation of workers is deserving of it.

Preface

Long before there were affinity groups, employment councils, and workforce diversity banding with scorecards, there were indicators of a changing workplace. Employers saw it first-hand, and studies presaged the fact that our workforce was aging, needing more technologically advanced skills, and becoming increasingly supplied with immigrants from all over the world. Anticipating these trends while operating in a global economy, employers began to plan for this new workforce — this more diverse workforce, different from anything ever seen before. But while most employers understood and satisfied their prescribed legal requirements to promote equal opportunity and ensure nondiscrimination in the workplace, the concept of "diversity" offered no such blueprint. And so the task of defining diversity and defending its business value fell upon each organizational leader.

Today, without a legal compliance mandate on diversity, there is still much variance as to how it is practiced, why it is important, and how much of a resource investment it should require. For those leaders who adopted diversity practices and made them an integral part of their organizational culture, their "aha!" moment came when they saw results; when diversity equaled profitability and sustainable success through greater workforce engagement. For those leaders, diversity became part of their culture of inclusion, which means accepting, valuing, and engaging everyone. Everyone had an opportunity to succeed. The business case for diversity is no different than the people case for diversity — they are one and the same. Simply put, open and unfettered access to all available human talent is the best way to find the best talent. And top talent produces top results. A trajectory that began with legal mandates for nondiscrimination and affirmative action has evolved into the recognition that talent cannot be drawn from just a select few groups, but rather expanded to envelop the richness of backgrounds, qualities, abilities, and experiences that every aspiring individual has to offer regardless of personal characteristics. A commitment to diversity and inclusion extends beyond legal constraints by proactively seeking such talent and opening all opportunities to them.

For many years, we have been encouraged by colleagues and friends to share our thoughts as to what will come next in the field of diversity. After all, through our combined experience, we have been fortunate enough to have influenced the evolution of equal employment opportunity and affirmative action programs and to have witnessed and been part of the emergence of multiculturalism, diversity, and inclusion, from different vantage points: as federal officials responsible for public policymaking in these programs and as private-sector executives, consultants, business owners, authors, and thought leaders. We have promoted the shift in emphasis, away from just counting heads toward making each head count, in our quest for attracting and making full use of our nation's diverse talent pool. If to go forward one must first look back, we certainly have that path well covered from various perspectives.

This book may well be about predicting the next big phase. But, it is a different type of book. It is not a business book. It is not an HR manual. It is not a legal treatise on diversity; nor is it a template for practicing diversity. There are plenty of books and other resources already available to provide specific guidance in these areas. Rather, this book is a hybrid of all these required elements of global leadership. It cuts across all of these elements while adding a few more. There is no one formula to follow, no specific best practices that must be adopted to ensure success. Instead, this book will encourage and guide you to tap into and rely on your inner resources — "your heart" — to make a lasting difference in the workplace. Leadership from the heart combines a strong functional knowledge and business acumen with the virtues that make us human: character, compassion, empathy, and integrity. Together, they make a powerful combination that can outlast and outperform any other method or legal prescription. HR professionals are pivotal to the success of this combination. They provide the bridge between the highest aspirations that exist within an organization and the application of daily efforts that will yield the desired results. Throughout the book you'll find examples of real-life conversations and situations to which we have been privy in our various capacities. Due to confidentiality and legal considerations, we are presenting these stories without attribution. Nevertheless, they are real and true to life.

Over the past couple of decades, we have seen an explosion of new words and expressions in the English language, reflecting the dramatic impact that the Internet, technology, globalization, and shifting demographics have had on our daily lives. Words such as "Google," "avatar," and "Sudoku," and phrases such as "speed dating" and "online shopping" are commonplace in conversations. Human Resources is no different, having added to our lexicon such terms as "glass ceiling," "broadbanding," and "onboarding." The speed of technology has allowed us to remain connected at all times, while reducing our messages to a handful of vowels and consonants — mere transactions. We don't seem to have time for more. Somehow, the heart has been left out of our busy daily interactions. The time has come to add to our rather extensive vocabulary of impersonal and technical terms one that involves the heart. The word is *"ganas"* (gah-nas).

For those that don't know, *ganas* is a Spanish word that speaks to one's inner motivation and drive. There might be other uses and applications of this word, but in its origin, the word means inspired motivation. In the context of diversity, *ganas* inspires us to work for fairness, equity, inclusion, and acceptance in all of our practices — not an isolated policy here or a networking event there. Inspired action moves the conversation from the mechanical, prescribed letter of the law toward the uplifting spirit of the law, aligning character, attitude, and ability with organizational objectives. Our message to you is simply this: Be diverse, responsive, and visionary in your workplaces by design, not by government mandates. Warding off discriminatory practices, as so many of you have done so well, isn't just about doing the right thing, or having good business sense, or about following the letter of the law. It is about bettering our workplaces, nurturing the spirit of our people, cultivating our people resources, and propelling us forward through the productivity and ingenuity of our talent. The aim is to forge policies within companies that are not only fair-minded, but also principled. Doing things right always transcends the pure letter of the law. The more advantageous focus is that of creating environments that are guided by moral, ethical, and equal opportunity principles and built on a foundation of fairness, openness, and accountability, as well as legal rights.

Former Justice Sandra Day O'Connor, the first woman to serve on the Supreme Court, observed before her retirement, "The power I exert on the court depends on the power of my argument, not on my gender."[1] Indeed, a key element of diversity is recognizing that talent has no relationship to factors like race or gender. Diversity is foremost about opportunity. In delivering the Court's ruling on a major landmark case involving race, Justice O'Connor further observed, "Effective participation by members of all racial and ethnic groups in the civic life of our Nation is essential if the dream of one Nation, indivisible, is to be realized … In order to cultivate a set of leaders with legitimacy in the eyes of the citizenry, it is necessary that the path of leadership be visibly open to talented and qualified individuals of every race and ethnicity."[2]

Keeping that path open is essential to fulfilling America's promise. But it is a task attainable only if it is shared and advanced by each and every one of us, regardless of rank or title. It can be done, and the HR professional's role must be instrumental in the process. We have seen these issues first-hand, and are proud to have assisted motivated employers along the way. This book is for all who are so inspired, but are looking for more guidance and direction in their efforts to achieve an inclusive and diverse workforce. For those who operate without policies, programs, or discussions surrounding diversity and inclusion, we hope this book serves as an inspirational starting point. For those who are embracing diversity through an isolated program or two such as supplier diversity, external hiring, or community outreach, we hope you are inspired to undertake a more comprehensive approach. And, for the employer and HR manager who have myriad practices and policies in place, perhaps there will not be a singular "aha" moment, but the inspiration to "check under the hood" to ensure that these practices are functioning well and producing the results intended.

We firmly believe in the power of each individual. We each have a responsibility to use our inner qualities to reach our goals and inspire those around us. Our motivation, our *ganas*, is the key to our success as individuals and as a nation.

01 Heartfelt Leadership

"The law can push open doors and tear down walls, but it cannot build bridges. That job belongs to you and me." — Thurgood Marshall[1]

Heartfelt Leader

The influential vice chairman of a financial services institution passively supported harassment prevention policies until one day his daughter came home totally distraught over the sexual harassment she was being subjected to within her workplace. He shared that this experience turned him into one of his company's most vigilant advocates for strong enforcement of policies prohibiting such behavior, demanding serious consequences for violators. *Policies are often strengthened through personal experience.*

Reform, Renew, Resolve.

We've heard these rallying cries over and over. When things go wrong, what appeals to the human spirit is a fresh start. Yet, ironically, to begin anew and lead in a different direction, the sources we must draw upon are not themselves new. They are timeless. Some might even call them "old-fashioned." They are qualities that inspire us to believe, to engage, and to attain. Everyone has them, but not everyone taps into them. Leaders who lead with their heart allow themselves to be guided by these forces.

We are talking about qualities of the heart: sincerity, integrity, and empathy. HR professionals are the keepers and advocates of these qualities in the workplace. They serve as the voice and conscience for translating good intentions into lasting organizational values. For all the business terms and concepts, it comes down to people, and how organizations treat, relate to, and include them. Recent experiences have shown that accounting principles are only sound when people's principles are sound. Corporate governance will not be fully optimal without workforce governance. The health of capital markets will succumb to illness and decay if we don't tend to the health of our human capital, which is ultimately the engine that drives our economy. Finally, if we are not diligent in the use, management, and inclusion of all our available human capital, then our workplaces become inefficient and unhealthy. HR professionals play a key role in bridging the aspirations for a full and inclusive workplace with the applications for results.

Leadership

There are as many different styles of leadership as there are leaders. Of all the characteristics that employers look for in individuals — characteristics such as communications skills, exceptional judgment and functional know-how, creativity, and team orientation — the one that is in greatest demand is leadership ability. Why? Because companies understand that they might gain short-term advantage through technology, service innovation, product development, mergers, or acquisitions, but they do not sustain that advantage without leaders. What do we mean by that? Organizations want individuals who can anticipate opportunities, set the course, inspire belief and commitment, rally support, and deliver results. Leadership, hard to define yet easy to identify, is that ability to move individuals and organizations to action. Leaders do not have to be at the head of the table in the boardroom, nor in the boardroom at all. Such leadership could come from the plant manager 350 miles from the regional headquarters and across the country from corporate, or from the HR manager assigned to a poorly performing product line — both working toward fostering the talents and desires of all toward a common purpose or goal. The achievement of diversity and inclusion most likely will take place through a series of finite, individual decisions and placements made at the local levels, rather than by mantras emanating from the C-suite.

Leadership experts tell us that in yesterday's world, the "numbers" and routine mechanics lulled us into thinking that we were fulfilling a purpose simply by repeating a formula. Repetition works well in an industrial setting, but not in a global economy driven by service and technology. A shift from management to leadership is one of outlook and attitude. Leadership moves us from rigidity to flexibility. It allows us to adapt in a more uncertain environment. Leadership urges people to take responsibility, to take initiative, to do the right things, and therefore to excel. Leadership is not exclusive to a few "top executives." It is open to all throughout the organization. It is not title or rank. Leadership is ownership.

Heartfelt leadership is the ability to guide and direct by drawing on those features and characteristics that are intrinsically human and noble. Having the skills, competencies, creativity, and expertise to lead, heartfelt leaders differ from the field in that they care and show they care. They lead by example. They understand that change is difficult and personally take on the mantle of ownership. Such leaders understand that the impetus for change starts at the top. Heartfelt leaders infuse, involve, and include others, all others: those who are in the mainstream and those who are in the peripheries. They relate to individuals at all levels of the organization and find ways to reach out to them. Heartfelt leaders don't look down to find common ground among diverse and divergent views; instead, they look up, inspiring others and elevating their sights toward a unifying vision of what is possible and achievable if everyone works together. This type of leader speaks to our hopes and ideals. Their vision of a united, inclusive workplace provides limitless opportunities for those who possess the talent, drive, and personal qualities to commit.

Management guru Dr. W. Edwards Deming, famous for thought leadership that has helped revolutionize companies and industries, once cautioned:

> "It is important that an aim never be defined in terms of activity or methods. It must always relate directly to how life is better for everyone."[2]

Heartfelt leaders provide personally empowering opportunities and capitalize on the moment, not by binding others to the rigidity of the laws, but by raising their level of effort toward a higher purpose: a better quality of work life and employee satisfaction for all.

Leadership with Integrity

At the core of such a leader is an unquestionable sincere heart, one that allows employees to forge on knowing that the helm is guided by honesty, with the employees' best interests at heart. While employees place a premium on sincerity and integrity, with one survey[3] reporting that it was "critical" or "important" that they work for an ethical company — 82 percent preferring to be paid less working for an ethical company than receiving a higher salary with a company whose ethics were questionable — the same is true for those just entering the workforce. Sincerity and integrity have moved to the forefront with the Millennial generation, who make up the recent college graduate population, as they place these qualities at the top of the list of corporate traits they are looking for in an employer — up from seventh only a few years ago.[4]

The magic of the holiday movie favorite "It's a Wonderful Life" rests with George Bailey (Jimmy Stewart) and his sincerity and understanding for not only his employees but also the people of Bedford Falls. Bailey, an empathetic leader with a solid moral compass, works tirelessly to help the citizens of Bedford Falls into home ownership. He does this because he genuinely cares about his community and the welfare of its residents. When Bailey falls on hard times and is on the verge of losing his business, he is embarrassed, becomes despondent, and considers taking his own life. Fortunately, his "inner voice," in the form of a ministering spirit, encourages him to return home, where he is welcomed back by many of those individuals he helped over the years. They were there for him just as he was there for them during difficult times. Sad to say, but many leaders fail to show their compassionate side until it is too late. They have not generated good will prior to their moment of need. This type of leader often finds no one there to go the extra mile for the company when needed. In contrast, the George Baileys of the world, whether facing natural disasters or inclement weather, delivery delays or economic tough times, discover that there are many hands willing and ready to help.

James A. Drake, president of Florida's Brevard Community College (BCC), serves as a real-life example of leadership with commitment. Drake, earning $190,000 a year (not much by college president standards), turned down his annual pay increase once again — for the third year running. Instead, Drake requested that his proposed $100,000 pay increase be donated back to the school to help defray the cost of textbooks for needy BCC students, as books are a major collegiate expense. Inspired by Drake's generosity, a local family came forward and initiated its own BCC scholarship. Similarly, the University of Pennsylvania announced that its president, Amy Gutmann, and her husband would donate $100,000 to support undergraduate research, another instance of leading by example. For years, Dr. B. Lyn Behrens, a pediatrician by training and the recently retired president and CEO of Loma Linda University and Medical Center, led with the same commitment, foregoing more lucrative opportunities and greater income potential for the sake of advancing the mission of an institution she dearly loved. Upon learning of her impending retirement, the outpouring of support, appreciation, and yes, even love for all she meant and sacrificed during her tenure came from all areas and levels, from both inside and outside the institution. Benevolent leadership speaks volumes to employees, customers, and the surrounding community. Some people are leaders because of the position they hold; others are leaders by their example.

This type of leadership becomes most evident when witnessing how employers treat their most valuable of all resources — the people they employ. More than just a passing feeling or emotion, the heartfelt leader's call to equality and fairness is so inherent that it permeates all transactions. For some leaders, the call for fairness comes naturally — they see things the way they should be, and are guided by their innate instincts, even if the examples around them are not worthy of emulation. For others, the evolution could have been more environmental — parents, guardians, teachers, or mentors molded their values and character. It might have been something as simple as *Leave the world a little better than you found it*. Each individual calibrates to a moral compass based on a different internal or external stimulus.

Examples abound of early corporate titans who led from the heart. Robert Wood Johnson, chairman of the Johnson & Johnson Company from 1932 until 1963, personally wrote the company's credo back in 1943. The credo outlines a set of guiding principles that have served as the company's operating framework ever since. It predates the Civil Rights Act of 1964, as well as the currently popular "corporate social responsibility" concept, and many other laws that regulate the workplace. Though the language has been updated over the years, its essence has remained constant. Among its corporate values, the credo states:

"We are responsible to our employees, the men and women

who work with us throughout the world. Everyone must be considered as an individual. We must respect their dignity and recognize their merit.... There must be equal opportunity for employment, development and advancement for those qualified. We must provide competent management, and their actions must be just and ethical."[5]

These values make up the DNA of the company's culture and serve to guide their decisions. The company has been tested time and again, as was the case during the Tylenol crisis of 1982, when bottles of Extra-Strength Tylenol were found tampered with and laced with cyanide, causing several deaths. The company quickly accepted responsibility for this crisis, even though the circumstances appeared to point elsewhere. It conducted a national recall of the product at a cost of millions and millions of dollars, and lived up to its values, earning the praise and respect of the corporate and consumer world, both nationally and internationally.

Similarly, IBM's corporate heritage, its roots, implanted a deep commitment to diversity from its inception. Reflecting on the company's rich history and commitment to diversity innovation, J. Randall MacDonald, IBM's senior vice president of human resources, commented,

"IBM hired women as early as 1899, twenty years before women were given the right to vote. That same year, we hired our first black employee, thirty-six years after the Emancipation Proclamation and ten years before the founding of the NAACP. And in 1914, we hired our first employee with a disability, seventy-six years before the Americans with Disabilities Act became law."[6]

The essence of these actions and values became codified in policy statements long before the passage of the Civil Rights Act of 1964. In fact, then-CEO Thomas J. Watson Jr. issued his first policy statement back in 1953, well before companies felt the active presence and oversight of regulators and civil rights advocates (see Figure 1.1). Over time, the company's statements have been revised to adapt to the changing times, yet the spirit of commitment to fairness that was evident in those early years continues to permeate throughout every expression and affirmation of these values.

Figure 1.1

INTERNATIONAL BUSINESS MACHINES CORPORATION
500 MADISON AVENUE
NEW YORK 22. N.Y.

OFFICE OF
THE PRESIDENT

Confidential   **September 21, 1953**

Policy Letter #4

The purpose of this letter is to restate for all of the supervisory personnel of the IBM Company the policy of this corporation regarding the hiring of personnel with specific reference to race, color, or creed.

Under the American system, each of the citizens of this country has an equal right to live and work in America. It is the policy of this organization to hire people who have the personality, talent and background necessary to fill a given job, regardless of race, color, or creed.

If everyone in IBM who hires new employees will observe this rule, the corporation will obtain the type of people it requires, and at the same time we will be affording an equal opportunity to all in accordance with American tradition.

T. J. Watson, Jr.

IBM's commitment to the individual, expressed in a progress report to employees in 1961, stated:

"… our fine reputation as a company is based on nothing more and nothing less — than respect for the individual, integrity and personal values of our people. You are, in fact, the IBM Company."

Driving Diversity by Active Engagement

"Like any effort, there is much room for improvement. My continued frustration is that it never seems to run on its own. I have to continually push the effort or it loses momentum." — An active CEO

Heartfelt leaders are not afraid to go it alone, regardless of industry or legal standards. Caring is at their core. They not only envision how things should be, but show the ability to communicate and navigate toward that goal, forging consensus and buy-in from executives and senior managers who might be resistant or even recalcitrant. They not only hold a vision of the future, but also envision how each employee can play a role in the realization of that goal. Integrity is at their core. Not only are they strong in their convictions, but also they are unwavering in their actions and follow-through. Success involves a cohesive, coordinated implementation strategy, coupled with an oversight plan that is driven by top leadership. Without such, words are simply that — words.

Heartfelt leaders know that it takes their active engagement in the process: consistency and persistency of message, follow-through, evaluation, and personal intervention, when appropriate. They fully appreciate that they must rely on others to manage and carry out their vision; yet, they possess an innate sense of responsibility, of ownership of the process, recognizing that they must take the initiative to guide the implementation plan. Pronouncements by fiat in a vacuum don't take hold in today's complex organizations, at least not in the successful ones.

Heartless Humor

"Looks like the new CEO's vision statement will hold up better than the last."

Every time a company is acquired, downsized, restructured, realigned, or the senior leadership is changed, a flurry of activity follows, often resulting in a new vision and mission statement. After its emergence, employees await guidance as to how to implement this newly pronounced direction and how they can assist in forging the new course. Employees hope that the values and culture articulated in the vision statement are meaningful and sincere, and not just a form of window dressing or a public relations ploy.

Leading by Example

A Case in Point

The incoming CEO of a multinational corporation, wanting to set the tone and make his mark on the company, set out to issue a new vision statement. Beautifully crafted, that statement clearly articulated his expectation of a workplace free from any kind of prejudice, bias, or discrimination, and welcoming of differences. Calling together his senior management team, the CEO discussed his commitment to equal opportunity and inclusion, and further affirmed that he would like to see people of color, women, and individuals with disabilities moving up within the corporate ranks. At a year-end corporate performance evaluation meeting, along with financial results and economic profit calculations, there was a report on executive talent development efforts, and another report relating to discrimination claims and settlements. These reports revealed a slight increase in discrimination charges, and only one woman and one person of color added to the roster of over 100 potential future executives. The CEO had been sincere in his desires; yet, not much had changed.

Much like the CEO in the "Case in Point" example, who relied solely on his pronouncements for diversity results, many executives might not be following through with a plan for action, standards for accountability, and measurable outcomes. A recent survey markedly depicts the existence of a gap, a disconnect between expectations and outcomes. The survey asked whether companies practice diversity in their workforces as much as they claim publicly. Only 22 percent of those surveyed said yes, while a resounding 78 percent said no! A large majority of workers believe that having a diverse workforce is something that most companies publicize far more than they actually implement — capturing the disconnect between words and deeds.[7] For some employers, a bigger gap exists between what they think is happening and what is really happening. As companies and other organizations struggle to compete and cast themselves as diversity leaders, the price they are paying has become almost prohibitive as they:

» financially support a variety of causes and social concerns;

» take out ads in journals and affinity publications that prominently feature their commitment to diversity;

» devote thousands of hours of executive management time and effort on meetings and targeted programs;

» join respected professional associations; and,

» invest considerable resources on diversity initiatives.

Yet, in spite of these costly undertakings, many continue to be frustrated with the slow pace of progress. The diversity disconnect is due in large part to the fact that this effort has been approached from the outside in rather than from the inside out. For some, external forces, such as legal prescriptions and competitors' "best practices," have been the stimulus for action, rather than allowing the organization's own guiding beliefs to serve as the impetus for change. The safe harbor theory proposes that if an employer checks all the boxes, does all it is told to do in regulations, and even borrows other employers' best practices, a great program would result. At a minimum, these employers should be found in legal compliance. While many are working hard to do just that, they could be satisfying the intent of the law without meeting its spirit. Employees, suppliers, and customers alike can easily detect variances between words and deeds. The heartfelt executive understands, as do employees, the vacuous nature of words in isolation. Such a leader knows that words of inclusion must be active. A passive approach allows too much room for neglect, disinterest, or outright distrust of anyone deemed different. Forging a path from within, rather than duplicating the practices in place in another company, industry, or city, allows the employer to focus on the hopes and desires, skills, and talents of his or her workforce — its starting point and its inclusive, diverse endpoint.

Many companies are known for their multiple awards and recognitions as equal opportunity employers. They are celebrated and honored by publications and associations. Others choose a quieter path, away from the limelight and fanfare. Kaiser Permanente (KP) is one of those honored, celebrated companies today, but it was not always this way. For years the company went at it alone, leading from the heart. This practice dates back to the mid 1940s when the company's founder, Henry J. Kaiser, made substantial contributions to the racial and ethnic diversity of the San Francisco Bay Area through the recruitment of black employees from the Southern States, Hispanics from the Southwest, and Asian immigrants from the West Coast to work in the shipyards of Richmond, California. Kaiser provided health care to the shipbuilding workforce as an employment benefit and delivered it in racially integrated facilities, a practice that ran counter to the prevailing practice in the community and most of the nation at that time. Despite considerable pressures from the medical community and some of the citizenry, Kaiser was steadfast in his conviction that segregated health care was not only illogical and unfair but also cost-inefficient. It made no moral or business sense to recruit people from diverse cultures and backgrounds to the workforce and then to treat them unfairly.

Today, KP is one of the nation's largest private providers of integrated health care services with approximately 8.7 million plan members and one of the health care industry's most diverse workforces at all levels and areas of employment. But KP's commitment to diversity goes beyond hiring and promotion issues to ensuring it is able to respond to the growing diversity of its customers. KP's National Diversity Agenda was designed to enhance its capability to deliver culturally competent care to an increasingly diverse membership; strategically increase the diversity of its workforce to meet customer needs; and grow membership in diverse markets, the fastest growing segments of the population. The end results are better communications across languages and cultures, and the reduction of health care disparities among targeted populations. This is all thanks to Henry Kaiser having a keen business sense and leading from his heart.

Giant Eagle is one of the largest privately held, family owned supermarkets in the United States. In existence since 1931, the company now has over 200 supermarkets and more than 35,000 employees. In 2005, Giant Eagle was presented with the Equal Employment Opportunity Commission's "Freedom To Compete" award in recognition of its highly successful efforts to train and employ students with disabilities. In recounting the humble origins of the company at the ceremony, Daniel Shapira, owner and special counsel, said the following:

> "There are five families who founded the company. Those five families were not related, but they had several things in common. The principal ones were that they came to this country from Europe and Russia, they spoke no English, and they had nothing on their backs besides their clothes. And this country gave them an opportunity — an equal opportunity — to compete fairly and freely. And as a result of this, they were able to build one of the true success stories in the United States. Because of the equal opportunity that the owners of this company had, they set up a credo that the company has operated under for all of its years, and that is to provide equal opportunity to all of its employees. ... I remember when I was three or four years old getting introduced to the issue of equal opportunity and racial discrimination issues, overhearing my father who was then the CEO of the company, talking to my mother about the fact that he wanted to hire African American truck drivers and that the Teamsters in those days were refusing to let him do that. And my father said, "We're

not going to have a company like that. We're going to take a strike or whatever else we have to do to beat that kind of attitude." And we have been one of the first and principal companies that broke the union barriers across all union lines in every market that we do business. My parents, if they were still alive, would be really smiling if they could see me up here accepting this award for them, because they lived their lives under the principles that this agency stands for, and we do not do projects to win awards. In this particular program being recognized, we've hired over 300 employees/ students, 150 of whom are still with us on a full-time or part-time basis, and many of whom have been with us for more than ten years."[8]

A Commitment to Fairness

Sincerity, empathy, integrity, and a sense of fairness, mixed with keen business acumen and innovation, have provided Giant Eagle with a winning recipe for success. That same call for fairness and justice was seen in December 2005, when The Gallup Organization released its findings of a public opinion poll conducted on the state of discrimination in the workplace. The survey found that employees who rated their company high on matters of diversity were, not surprisingly, more positive about their workplace, more likely to remain with their company, and more likely to recommend it to others. Specifically, the poll revealed that persons working for companies that scored highly on questions of diversity were twice as satisfied with their work experiences than were employees who worked for companies with a lesser tangible commitment to diversity. When employees perceive that the head of their organization has a strong commitment to diversity, they are more than twice as likely to be satisfied with their workplace, and their retention is almost a third higher.[9] The resounding message in the Gallup findings was this: The American worker wants a workplace where the commitment to diversity begins at the top and permeates throughout.

Most companies' roots began with a few individuals having a focused ideal, a vision, or a talent that united them. Whatever the industry or sector, company founders share a strong commonality and sense of purpose. As the business grows, so too do the employment opportunities for others with a different skill mix and diversity in culture, race, and gender. The heartfelt leader listens, acknowledges that transformation is required, and takes action. Such a leader will work to ensure that diversity and inclusion are internalized, integrated, and reflected throughout future expansion efforts. Knowing that what works in one business line, unit, or office might not be as successful in another due to different starting points, cultures, or business requirements, the heartfelt leader expects all managers to tailor these efforts to their own specifications.

By forging partnerships within and throughout, where all employees know the commitment to and value of diversity, a greater sense of ownership will result. When a path or a strategy is not reaping the intended results, heartfelt leaders encourage the gleaning of the best of what's working and march on, shoulder-to-shoulder. With the vigilant oversight of the C-suite and accountability up and down the ranks, line managers and employees alike will understand that it is their concerted efforts that will yield lasting economic and social results. They will also recognize and take full advantage of the support and affirmation that the well-intentioned executive ranks can provide. Moving beyond good intentions to deeds and actions takes motivation and a strong desire. *"Ganas"* is that call to action.

But let's be clear: Being a heartfelt leader doesn't mean that you have to leave your business acumen at the front door. Quite the contrary, it means that you complement your business acumen with the internal qualities that will set you apart from other organizations. What will be discussed in this book will make it more likely that your organization will succeed.

02 Got *Ganas?* Leading by Inspiring

"Leadership is not so much about technique and methods as it is about opening the heart. Leadership is about inspiration — of oneself and of others. Great leadership is about human experiences, not processes. Leadership is not a formula or a program, it is a human activity that comes from the heart and considers the hearts of others. It is an attitude, not a routine." — Lance Secretan[1]

Heartfelt Leader

A CEO of the U.S. operations of a European company became convinced of the value of diversity when the company converted the concept into a branding opportunity and a marketing advantage. The marketplace began to associate this company not only with quality service but also with an aggressive commitment to diversity and inclusion. This new reputation offered significant benefits in terms of the diverse top talent wanting to work there and the increased business opportunities that such recognition generated. *There is a business case for diversity for those willing to reach out.*

Laissez Faire. Kaizen ... *Ganas.*

Many foreign words and terms enter the English language to convey a certain process, policy, or character quality difficult to express otherwise. The time has come to add to the business lexicon a word that captures a new attitude, a new style of leadership. The word is *"ganas."* A Spanish word, *ganas* (gah-nahs) has no literal English translation; yet, it describes perfectly the concept of inspired motivation. In the Spanish language, it is used for all kinds of things: a father teaching his daughter to swing at a baseball might say, *"dale con ganas"* (hit the ball with *ganas*); a teenager being asked to do chores around the house might reply *"cuando me lleguen las ganas"* (when the *ganas* come to me) or, worse, *"no tengo ganas"* (I don't have any *ganas*). There might be other applications and associations with the word *ganas*, but in its true meaning, the word captures the animating spirit within each person.

Ganas speaks to the inner desire to succeed. It is inspired leadership. It generates action. Inspired action elevates our thinking in the midst of uncertainty and drives behavior toward the pursuit of excellence in the treatment of others. *Ganas* encourages each individual to align character and attitude with skills and experience. It is about pursuing ideals that motivate to achieve greatness. Such motivation has been known to be a key driver in high performers. Talent is nothing without motivation. Talent determines aptitude but inspired motivation (*ganas*) determines altitude. Abraham Lincoln had *ganas*; Martin Luther King Jr. had *ganas*. Great leaders look beyond the immediate challenges to the full potential of an opportunity. President Lincoln envisioned a nation united in purpose and ideals. He could see the possibilities beyond the clear and present danger of a civil war. The opportunity of liberty and freedom for all would serve as the underpinning of a long-lasting and peaceful union. Martin Luther King Jr. envisioned the economic, social, and political potential of a nation where people would be judged by their character and not by the color of their skin. As he often mentioned in his speeches, Martin Luther King Jr. could see the "mountain top." Transformational leaders can look into the future and envision the benefits to be gained. They envision possibilities that elevate others.

What do leaders with *ganas* do? They possess a higher order way of thinking. They speak to common purpose and shared values. They understand that change is hard to come about. It takes perseverance, passion, and even pain. Change leadership starts at the top. All the companies that have had lasting results in terms of social change, economic progress, or in their diversity efforts have had CEOs that have taken ownership of the process. These leaders accept and stand ready to face the challenges. They inspire others to follow suit while setting high standards and requiring accountability of effort. There will always be reasons to delay or prolong making a decision. For example, passing over some individuals for a bonus or stock grant, or making others wait just a bit longer for a promotion or stretch assignment until the timing is "just right." But, the concept of *ganas* inspires leaders to accept and include, to develop and promote, to take some risks and to reward equitably across the board. Understanding that one will never have perfect information, the leader with *ganas* knows he or she must act in the absence of certainty. It's about aligning character and attitude with organizational success. An indomitable spirit to aspire, to lead, and to contribute can far outweigh the minimalist expectations of the law.

Anyone can have *ganas*. It is an equal opportunity desire that, when tapped, can drive an individual to action, and, when left dormant, can deprive a leader of a valuable asset. The challenge is to decide whether to ignore that inner sense of desire — in this context, the desire for workplace fairness and inclusion — or whether to tap one's *ganas* to work toward inclusion at all levels and in all areas of employment.

B.D. — Before Diversity

Affirmative action efforts of the past and present, without inspiration, constrain us to the numbers and routine mechanics of counting one of this protected group and two of the other.

Indeed, prescribed affirmative action efforts are by their very nature limited in scope and results. They often do not foster awareness or greater understanding of organizational impediments, bias, or developmental partiality.

A Case in Point

As an EEO officer for a growing company that supplies janitorial services to the federal government, Terry struggles with just how to report affirmative action updates to senior management. Terry knows that the company is hiring from more diverse pools than ever before and that the company is firmly committed to individual contributions, inclusion and diversity. Senior management also reviews diversity by professional bands and by organizational units on a quarterly basis. When Terry runs the numbers using the federal government's required affirmative action job groupings, there are shortfalls in progress. Worse, the government-mandated job groups and corporate diversity bands do not mesh. The company's bands make more business sense and are a better reflection of career progression. Yet, Terry has to brief management the way the federal government's investigators want the data, in the fashion they require, regardless of practicality or purpose.

Political changes, buffeted by public opinion, bring about swift shifts in public policy. Such changes often produce policy reversals. This can be seen in a historical review of the American experience with affirmative action: new presidential executive orders superseding existing ones, new regulations replacing the old, new and different processes, and a variety of accountability measures and methodologies for yet even more numbers-counting. This push-pull, fall back, and spring forward approach has reduced affirmative action efforts to a technical level of compliance often tended to in a vacuum.

For example, employers that have federal contracts are required to develop and maintain affirmative action plans as a condition of their doing business with the government. Most employers will acknowledge that they keep two sets of books. The first set is for "the government," written in the technical language that will pass muster during an audit or investigation. This set of books has little if any connection to the organization's day-to-day operational objectives or long-term strategic goals. The second set of books uses language, guidance, and descriptions that are more closely aligned with the organization's culture and stated objectives. Written in company language, this second set makes the business case for diversity in a manner that will resonate with employees and will drive results. This programmatic divide has caused many employers to separate their affirmative action/regulatory compliance function away from their diversity initiatives, thus creating a less-than-ideal situation for staff involved in the coordination of both efforts.

Diversity and Inclusion

Achieving results beyond compliance to a sustained high level of workplace diversity and inclusion, however, requires increased understanding and an overt recognition that things can, and ought to, change. Inspired action does not confine itself to the rigidity of any law; rather, it transcends those boundaries, raising its standards to a higher level of conduct for the greater good, regardless of shifts in policy or regulatory technicalities. When numbers alone are the focus, cohesion and relevance to organizational structure and business goals could be lacking. Sustainable achievements in diversity result from its full and complete integration into all facets of employment.

The *Ganas* Gauge

When it comes to implementation, individuals possess different levels of motivation. Some might be completely satisfied running a basic, compliance-focused EEO program, while scores of others go much further, initiating a culture of diversity that involves training, affinity groups, and diverse suppliers. Undoubtedly, there are still some who prefer not to address diversity, though this pool is small and shrinking. Whether motivated by a personal situation such as a relative who has experienced unlawful discrimination or sexual harassment, or a legal proceeding requiring diversity training and other initiatives as remedial actions, employers often arrive at the same place from very different emotional and programmatic starting points. The *Ganas* Gauge (see Figure 2.1) offers a visual display of the range of motivational leadership that exists in a workplace. At one end of the Gauge, there are those who have no intellectual or emotional investment in ensuring internal equity or inclusion; they are running on "Empty." At the other extreme are those running on "Full" — full of conviction and commitment. These individuals have been able to successfully institutionalize a culture of diversity, and believe it to have enhanced their profitability and competitive standing. Today, we find that most employers fall somewhere in the middle of the Gauge.

Figure 2.1

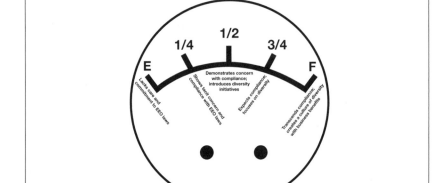

GANAS GAUGE

But, sound motives and good intentions will get a company only so far. Unless *ganas* for such is put into action and institutionalized, diversity efforts and initiatives can falter or die on the vine. Having a commitment to the principles of diversity and equal employment opportunity does not guarantee legal compliance with the myriad laws and regulations. Even the companies mentioned in this book, with their deeply committed leadership, have experienced employee transgressions and impermissible conduct. Their sheer size, with multiple collections of workers from disparate backgrounds and perspectives, can make it extremely challenging to ensure consistency in behaviors and harmony of views. Heartfelt leaders know this, but forge on, undeterred, picking employees up and bringing them along. While keeping ever vigilant about legal mandates and obligations, such employers elevate their focus beyond compliance to a higher level of principles and ideals that affirm the unique value of each individual and inspire their pursuit. At times, they surround themselves with like-minded committed individuals; at other times, they encourage and inspire others to hear and heed the call themselves. Examples of leaders operating with the *Ganas* Gauge on "Full" follow.

Frank Perez's Personal Involvement

Frank J. Perez is chairman of the Kettering Medical Center Network, which is a statewide consortium of hospitals and health care centers based in Kettering, Ohio. He carries a journal, which contains his personal and professional mission statements. In it, he describes how he guides his actions by his beliefs. This includes:

- » being a role model for others;
- » contributing positively to his field of endeavor;
- » building relationships that are important to the delivery of health care in the communities served; and,
- » being a source of support and encouragement to his family.

Perez has reached the pinnacle of his profession through an unlikely path, but not an uncommon one for many immigrants. He fled Cuba and arrived in the United States at the age of 18, joining his three sisters and mother who had come a year earlier. His father was not allowed to leave for another five years. In Cuba, Perez had dropped out of high school to avoid having to join the Communist Youth Militia. Now in the States, Perez found himself as head of the household, helping his mom and three younger sisters make ends meet. Working multiple jobs didn't allow him the luxury of attending a high school. So he signed up for correspondence courses and earned his high school diploma. Perez continued to pursue higher education, ultimately obtaining a master's degree in health care administration from George Washington University in Washington, D.C.

Over the past thirty years, Perez has led several hospitals, directing their growth and ensuring the best delivery of health care for the communities served. He is widely recognized within the health care industry as an innovative and inspiring leader, and as a health care executive who has fostered and promoted diversity in the development of talent. He has built one of the most diverse management teams in the industry and is credited for personally being able to attract top talent from major health care systems across the United States. Many of those he recruited have stated that they came to Kettering because of Perez's leadership style, his personal involvement with employees at all levels of the organization, and his dedication to people development. David Seidel, a longtime employee of Kettering, describes Perez's style in this way: "He picks what he thinks are good people, good leaders, even though they might be green ... he kind of hangs with them and gives them a nudge every once in a while."[2] Reflecting on his active pursuit of diverse talent, Perez commented in a featured article,

> "A lot of good people were willing to mentor and encourage
> me along the way. I believe I owe the next generation of

leaders that same degree of attention and care ... we need leaders who are magnets and mentors. If you have diverse leadership, it encourages younger minority executives to feel accepted and to trust that leadership. ... Celebrate diversity ... respect and enjoy different people, beliefs, values and ideas. I think that has allowed me to succeed."[3]

Frank Perez doesn't follow his heart; he leads with it. So does Julie Gilbert.

Julie Gilbert's WOLF Initiative

Julie Gilbert is a senior vice president with Best Buy Co., Inc. who heads retail training, leadership development, and Best Buy's global innovation engine. Just as important, Gilbert is the creator of Best Buy's WOLF (Women's Leadership Forum) initiative. Raised in South Dakota, Gilbert recalls growing up to the sounds of wolves or coyotes howling in the night. Once, she had a dream that woke her up in the middle of the night. In the dream, she heard those familiar sounds but instead of wolves or coyotes, the sounds came from voices of women. "Inspiration struck me, and I realized that each of us feels alone like a stray wolf, but if we are loyal like wolves are to each other, and we bond together with other females, we can reinvent the company and the industry, and we can build amazing leadership skills in the process."[4]

Best Buy's WOLF initiative captures the unique attributes that wolves possess. Here's how the company describes those attributes:

» Wolf Eyes. You never forget the eyes of a wolf ... they are focused on you authentically, piercing, and intense. The fundamental belief is that if leaders showed this type of "wolf eye" focus with each other, they would be more sharing and collaborative, and, in the process, would become more receptive to creative and innovative work.

» Wolf Loyalty. Wolves are very loyal to each other. In fact, they are one of the most loyal creatures in the animal kingdom.

» Wolf Teamwork. Wolves work in packs/groups/teams through cooperation and collaboration versus competing against each other.

» Wolves Engage. Wolves do not just "walk on by" a wolf pup that is struggling.

» Wolves Value Diversity. In documented studies of wolves, it has been shown that wolves will reach out to a stray wolf, pull it in, and help get it back on its feet (offering food, shelter, protection, etc.) In many cases, these formerly "stray" wolves become the alpha wolf, ensuring the pack has genetic diversity going forward since they generally stay together for generations.

» Wolves Bond. They form strong relationships with each other and in many cases are together for generations in wolf packs.

» Wolves Give Back. They always have at least one alpha wolf that shepherds and teaches each of them and links them with others when they need help.

» Wolves Leave Legacies. They make the environment they are in a better place — they give back.

And so Julie Gilbert believed that if women were encouraged to develop those unique wolf-like attributes — being supportive, nurturing the wolf pups (younger women), linking together as wolves do, and giving back to their "territory" (communities) — there would be no limits to what could be accomplished. The WOLF initiative is grounded in three pillars — commitment, networking, and giving back. As a result of this effort, Best Buy has dramatically increased its representation of women at the managerial levels: up 40 percent in the general managers category; 100 percent in the sales managers category; and 200 percent in women serving as district managers.[5] More than 20,000 Best Buy employees are now involved in this movement, creating "wolf packs" throughout the United States and Canada, and building partnerships with community groups and organizations at the local, national, and international levels.

Mark Nagel, Best Buy's director of Government Employment Practices, insightfully describes how the company has been able to combine Gilbert's high-level inspiration with practical, grassroots diversity efforts:

"Building diversity into the culture of a company is no small feat. So many times companies try to use posters, flyers, and websites to tell their employees "Look, we are diverse." I am proud that within Best Buy we chose to embrace diversity and build it into the fabric of the company. Within the culture of Best Buy, it is obvious that the message to each employee is that they must feel free to "bring their entire self to work." It is only through that being accomplished that individuals will be able to release their talents and add their own personal strand to the Best Buy tapestry.

How do you inspire each individual to bring that whole self? Again, build it into the "fabric" of the company:

Development — start with people not with posters
People inside Best Buy get opportunities throughout the year to sit with their respective supervisor and discuss goals, aspirations, talents, and skills they want to develop. This can lead to jobs or projects outside their department or into new areas of the company. Passion and encouragement often lead employees to positions they would have never imagined or previously didn't exist.

Values — words that speak to your core
Best Buy has clear values that speak to respecting what diversity brings to the company. At Best Buy, two of the four values speak directly to that:

» Unleash the power of your people, and

» Learn from challenge and change.

The values are not just words — they are discussed openly and seen as foundational in all talent discussions.

Supporting programs — Create an infrastructure that supports what builds from within
Employee Business Networks and specialized diversity training are foundational to help employees discover and build what diversity at Best Buy means to them. Also, a special program called WOLF was started by someone who did "bring their entire self to work" and championed her vision into a program to develop women within the company — now 20,000 strong — and changed the shopping experience for the female consumer within Best Buy.

Affirmative action is taught not as a compliance "bolt on" but as an enabler to the diversity work within the organization and an opportunity to examine applicant pools and how they can be impacted to reflect the communities that we serve."[6]

A dream, an inspiration for inclusion, coupled with the grassroots support of thousands who bought into that inspiration not only transformed a culture but also sizably increased Best Buy's market share by two percent (on $2.2 billion in revenues).[7] That would be a great ending to the story, but there's more. Gilbert's vision and internal initiative has moved beyond Best Buy toward a global network of women giving back to their communities and supporting mutual efforts. "So what started as one lone wolf howling in the night four years ago has become an empowering network — because women all over the world pricked up their ears and howled back."[8]

How do visionary leaders with the desire to leave a lasting legacy of inclusion do it? How do they summon their *ganas*, their inspiration, to begin to change a culture? How does one translate a vision into reality? The first operational step lies in *communicating* that vision.

03 Speaking from the Heart: Effective Communications

"If one is out of touch with one's self, one cannot touch others…
What matters is that one be for a time inwardly attentive."
— Anne Morrow Lindbergh[1]

Heartfelt Leader

A federal audit we led that looked into the employment policies and practices of a *Fortune* 500 company revealed certain promotional discrepancies. It found that the men who had been recently promoted into its senior executive ranks had received the corporate titles pertaining to the position — e.g., SVP or EVP — while the two women similarly promoted had not been awarded such titles. When presented with this discrepancy, the lead executive explained that the company was certain of the men's potential to grow into those roles, but wanted to determine whether the women could perform at those levels before granting the titles. Such candid comments led to a lengthy discussion of promotional standards, performance measures, nondiscrimination, and the chilling effect that the lack of a title would have on the women's ability to lead. A short time later, a hand-written note from the CEO arrived in the mail, informing us that the women had been awarded the appropriate corporate titles. *Adding a different, persuasive perspective to an issue and being willing to talk things through can often produce the desired outcome.*

Inform. Inspire. Impart.

Sincerity of message is more important than prose, style, or delivery. Integrity combined with an action plan reinforces authority. Do-as-I-say-and-not-as-I-do speakers lose face and followers. Therefore, any meaningful effort to effect change and rally support for the change must begin with a heartfelt message, one that is genuine, sincere, and authentic.

Management at all levels can be linked and united in focus and purpose through effective communications. It is one of the vital forces management has to successfully transform a workplace culture. A manager or supervisor at the local levels of an organization can draw upon the message conveyed by the CEO to drive performance and deliver results. One recent study by Watson Wyatt Worldwide captured this sentiment in its survey of almost 300 companies worldwide. The study found that those companies that communicated most effectively had higher total return to shareholders, and that effective communications was a driver of productivity rather than a result of strong financial performance.[2]

There is power and calibration in harkening back to the strategies and stated values that emanate from the top leadership. An important role for HR professionals is to strengthen the link between the C-suite and the rest of the organization by reaffirming the stated expectations and ensuring that day-to-day actions and behaviors match those expectations and further the mission.

Written statements and formal administrative guidance will assist in and should be used for the dissemination of policies and procedures. But the aspiration of an inclusive, fully participatory workforce calls for the use of more personal and direct forms of communication. Thanks to technology, communications can now take a host of vehicles. The formal workplace communications of yesterday — annual meetings, written policy directives, and hierarchical memos — have been replaced by, or expanded with, conference calls, instant messages, kiosk streams, web-based seminars, web town hall meetings, video conferencing, text messages, and e-mails. Newer forms of communications such as Internet social networks, blogs, and Twitter await. Different situations call for the use of different messaging devices. A heartfelt leader understands this and will tap whatever communications instrument is appropriate to engage others and convey the message that the thoughts, ideas, and successes of employees count and, in fact, are vital to the success of the company. Some of these communications differences are considered to be generational. However, the Twittering that reportedly went on with a dozen senior government officials during one of President Barack Obama's first nationally televised addresses (February 24, 2009)[3] proves otherwise.

It is critical to build a culture of transparency in which successes or setbacks, no matter how large or small, are communicated and shared. Employers that keep the workforce informed of initiatives, as well as their progress or disappointing results, build workplace cohesion and a heightened sense of purpose and trust. Conversely, employees that learn of economic or legal issues concerning their employer via the Internet or newspaper will be left with a sense of distrust. In these situations, employees might begin to question an employer's loyalty and honesty, and the "we" might erode quickly as employees focus on themselves, their livelihood, and their future. Communications expert Rene Henry states that not properly communicating with employees is one of the biggest mistakes any employer can make and offers that "Everyone must be on the same page, saying the same thing. An uninformed employee is dangerous."[4] Henry offers that there are many ways to stay in touch:

» An intranet, that can be accessed by employees only;

» A special telephone number for employees to retrieve important messages;

» Newsletters and other publications (hard copy and electronic);

» E-mails to all employees;

» Voicemail messages to employees;

» General assemblies and town hall meetings with employees; and,

» That personal one-on-one meeting.

Embracing the use of technology, Hershey Entertainment & Resorts (HE&R) undertook a transformation of its intranet services to foster a culture of openness and transparency as it automated many of its HR functions and corresponding communications.

" … [I]t shows we are meeting our goal of providing the workforce with the information they need — when they need it — along with the ability to share information on decisions with significant others in the home."[5]

Also using technology to reach its employees far and wide on HR issues, the CEO of online shoe and accessory store Zappos used his popular blog to reassure employees and outline steps the company was taking when it was forced to reduce its staff due to an economic downturn.

One corporate leader using a host of tools to communicate diversity progress to employees is Ryder Systems, Inc. For over 75 years, Ryder has been a leader in providing global transportation, logistics and supply chain management solutions. *InternetWeek* has named Ryder as one of the top 100 companies for its effective use of the Internet to achieve business results.[6] The same is true of Ryder's diversity initiatives. The core values of integrity, openness, and accountability for one's actions are at the heart of the company's diversity efforts. Chairman and CEO Gregory T. Swienton believes that "changing times call for a dynamic, diverse, multi-disciplined workforce that embraces change, new ideas, and collaborative problem solving."[7] The benefits of diversity and inclusion of a multicultural workforce have provided competitive advantages that help Ryder remain a strong industry leader. Utilizing the monthly employee magazine for spotlighting specific advancements and results, as well as using the Internet to broadcast initiatives and achievements to all employees helps keep inclusion and diversity at the forefront, rather than it becoming a once-a-year discussion.

There are still employment settings where communications is lacking. When this is the case, notices, directives, or even visits from corporate, regional, or divisional offices could be met with skepticism and discontent, indicative of a strained relationship between the executive leadership and those at the local levels of employment. Employees in this type of relationship might believe that senior management views them as a replaceable part and not as a vital, engaged partner. High turnover, lower productivity, unanswered employee relations issues, and poor morale are consequences directly resulting from such dysfunctional disconnects. In these situations, increased communications, emphasizing a common goal based upon mutual interdependence, is critical. Direct intervention, including more personal contact and frequent executive management and HR visits, might be required to change the culture and build trust in these settings. HR professionals can greatly assist by serving as a conduit of information, providing feedback to both sides of the communications spectrum, restoring energy, and placing focus on the shared organizational goals and objectives.

Top-Down Commitment

Rarely, if ever, does a cultural transformation occur without the direct and committed engagement of the top organizational leader. The chief executive must visibly and comfortably wear the mantle of building a workforce that is fully diverse and inclusive if others are to embrace such values. A singular manager might effect change in his or her unit by treating all employees with fairness, hiring from diverse employment pools, and developing and promoting talented employees while embracing their differences and unique skill mix. However, in almost all instances, the extent and results of such an effort will be localized and limited to the manager's area(s) of responsibility. The heartfelt senior executive, capitalizing on the authority of the position encumbered, can leverage that power to forge sweeping change. The key is institutionalizing that vision through communications and innovative practices.

A *Ganas*-led Leader

» Affirms the value of diversity at every opportunity;
» Aligns the principles of diversity with policies and practices; and
» Advances diversity through personal action.

The KnowledgeWorks Foundation, which is dedicated to improving the quality of high school education across the United States, coined the word VUCA. This term speaks to our changing world becoming increasingly ruled by Volatility, Uncertainty, Complexity, and Ambiguity (VUCA). While VUCA focuses on education, these same conditions apply to the workplace. In this world, employees must be engaged and encouraged to move beyond the rote requirements of their job descriptions and become a part of the solution, every solution, in an environment that is dynamic, fluid, uncertain, and complex.

Engagement and even emotional attachment to the organization involves a lot of factors, but a big part of it is feeling that your voice counts and someone is prepared to invest in you. If people feel they are growing, thriving, and making contributions that are recognized wherever they sit in the organization, they are more likely to give that discretionary effort, which is becoming critical for success.[8]

For those employers who hold federal contracts, listening to that inner voice will move them beyond the legal requirements to a much more substantive, less prescribed dialogue in which diversity and inclusion efforts are discussed, not to meet a requirement but rather to instinctively promote better solutions.

Heartfelt leaders must have a strategy when undertaking their communications campaign. Steve Reinemund, the retired chairman and CEO of PepsiCo, is one such leader. He made sweeping changes using a variety of communication strategies to convey his "6 P's" of Leadership. Reinemund's philosophy, in no specific order, requires:[9]

1. Principles: Possessing a moral compass as a leader.
2. Perspective: Dreaming and a vision, which leads to strategic planning.
3. Passion: A motivating commitment to what one does.
4. Perseverance: Sticking with it through the good and bad times.
5. Performance: Understanding that results matter.
6. People: Developing people is critical to successful leadership.

Reinemund not only told his employees of his philosophy that people development is critical to organizational success, but also told them again, and again. Having told employees of his vision, he puts it into action. "If you can't build the people, if you can't leave an organization stronger than you found it, with more capable people than you inherited, then I question whether you are adding value." Citing people who aided him along the way, since the second grade, Reinemund credits mentors with making him who and what he is today.[10] This belief led Reinemund to create PepsiCo's Leadership Development Program, which offers career development and credential building experiences for those in or near the executive ranks. That philosophy is communicated through personal action as well. Reinemund personally taught a class each year for a subset of middle managers. He led by example, signaling the importance of development for both business and people growth.

Using a variety of media to communicate principles and values reinforces the message and leads to greater cohesion and adherence to such tenets. For example, Procter & Gamble's values statement is specific and straightforward (see Figure 3.1). Following through on that articulated commitment is their succession planning process, which identifies talent for leadership development positions, including women and professionals of color. The company also maintains a formal mentoring program; encourages the formation of affinity groups; and monitors all of its employment practices, including hiring, promotion, and compensation, to ensure a fair and equitable process. Rather than simply a tagline as to being an equal opportunity employer, committed employers provide specifics and share their successes.

On the other side of the spectrum are employers who are silent on their tenets and guiding beliefs. No mention of the importance of treating individuals with dignity and respect. No talk of open and inclusive practices. No recognition of the value that employees add to the business. Reportedly, 42 percent of *Fortune* 50 companies' annual reports or social responsibility reports do not include a report on diversity efforts.[11] A review of the websites of the "fastest growing companies" in America shows that many have yet to articulate their founding principles and tenets. Such omission does not necessarily translate into lack of interest or commitment to these ideals. It can, however, raise questions for investors and prospective employees, especially Millennial generation workers who are mission connected and want to be part of a values-driven organization. Seeing a dearth of women and people of color on corporate boards year after year, stockholders are beginning to use their proxy statements as a way to influence change.[12]

Additionally, diversity efforts make good business sense for shareholders. Just ask Alan Mulally, CEO of Ford Motor Company. "Ford is a global business. We have a lot of talented people working together, and our performance will be determined by the breadth and depth of our inclusion of all our people. The more we embrace our differences within Ford — diversity of thought, experience,

Figure 3.1

OUR VALUES

P&G is its people and the values by which we live. We attract and recruit the finest people in the world. We build our organization from within, promoting and rewarding people without regard to any difference unrelated to performance. We act on the conviction that the men and women of Procter & Gamble will always be our most important asset.

Integrity

- We always try to do the right thing.
- We are honest and straightforward with each other.
- We operate within the letter and spirit of the law.
- We uphold the values and principles of P&G in every action and decision.
- We are data-based and intellectually honest in advocating proposals,
  including recognizing risks.

Leadership

- We are all leaders in our area of responsibility, with a deep commitment to deliver leadership results.
- We have a clear vision of where we are going.
- We focus our resources to achieve leadership objectives and strategies.
- We develop the capability to deliver our strategies and eliminate organizational barriers.

Ownership

- We accept personal accountability to meet the business needs, improve our systems and help others improve their effectiveness.
- We all act like owners, treating the Company's assets as our own and behaving with the Company's long-term success in mind.

Passion for Winning

- We are determined to be the best at capabilities and intentions.
- We believe that people work best when doing what matters most.
- We have a healthy dissatisfaction with the status quo.
- We have a compelling desire to improve and to win in the marketplace.

Trust

- We respect our P&G colleagues, customers, consumers, and treat them as we want to be treated.
- We have confidence in each other's capabilities and intentions.
- We believe that people work best when there is a foundation of trust.

perspective, race, gender, faith, and more — the better we can deliver what the customers want, and the more successful Ford will be. My priority is to ensure that inclusion at Ford is at the highest level of performance so that we include all employees deeply, thoughtfully, and broadly in the business."[13] An engaged HR team can capture the essence of such organizational values and encourage discussion and ultimately adoption of those principles in a public way.

What happens when the employer does not speak of its human resources as an integral component of success? What is the view of management when there is no direct communication with the employee due to size of the entity, location, or lack of appropriate technology? What happens when formal communications do not motivate or inspire, or seem to conflict with the way business is conducted? HR professionals can identify these shortcomings and provide the link to bridge the communications gap. At the local levels, human resources can generate interest and support, independent of these communications gaps by keeping line leadership informed of issues taking place both inside and outside of the organization. An employee of color being recognized by an outside group, or the departure of a high-performing employee with a disability can create opportunities to jump start communications. HR professionals can drive incremental change through their knowledge of and insight into the diversity dynamics facing the organization. Their position empowers them to serve as the voice for access and inclusion when senior leadership is either disengaged or distracted with other issues. Of course, this is not the ideal setting for an effective alignment of practices. Top-down communications from the C-suites to its U(under)-suites, and frequent feedback back up are vital if *ganas* for diversity is to become fully embedded in the culture.

The Mighty Middle

Downsizing and rightsizing activities of the past few decades have led to flatter organizations. In the 1980s, organizations streamlined their management ranks, broadening the scope of responsibilities and authority of those that remained. Middle managers occupy a difficult position in organizational hierarchies. They are sandwiched in between the exclusive senior executive ranks and the army of workers operating at the local levels. To them falls the difficult task of breaking broad, strategic goals into small, actionable steps. They interpret guidance, overlay their own views on stated principles, and create customized reward and recognition programs to drive performance. This group is expected to link the aspirations of the few at the top with the perspiration of the many in the trenches. Indeed, they hold posts that are both powerful and precarious.

Middle managers often find themselves competing for scarce resources and access to face time with the C-suite, while encountering increased pressures to produce more. When results are lacking, middle managers are far more vulnerable to being managed out or reassigned. But when profits and productivity are high, this group is empowered. They are often perceived as the "gatekeepers," deciding who gets seen and heard by senior executives, who gets selected for rotational and developmental assignments, and who makes the cut into the pool of high potentials. Ensuring a workplace supportive and inclusive of diversity may or may not be a priority goal at this level. It depends on many things. It depends on whether the middle manager truly believes that his or her superiors are actively engaged and committed to this goal. It depends on whether the middle manager is insecure of his or her own standing in the organization and counters by limiting access and inclusion of others. It also depends on whether the middle manager is personally committed to the pursuit of access and inclusion for all, regardless of company practice.

The mighty middle holds the key to both progress and plateaus. Consequently, these positions become crucial to the success of corporate-wide diversity efforts. HR professionals, working closely with these managers can assess the situation by seeking answers to these key questions:

» Is progress being made? If not, why?

» Is it purely due to competing demands?

» Is it poor communications as to what the goal of diversity "means" or that the goal "matters"?

» Is the lack of inclusion due to miscommunication?

» Is it due to fear?

» Or, is it attitudinal bias?

Once an evaluation is made, the HR professional can work with the manager to educate, inform, allay concerns, overcome obstacles, and restore balance. Human Resources is in a unique position to share ideas and successes across company-specific business lines and work units. Successes can proliferate or diminish due to culture, business lines, and even location. Human Resources can serve as a repository of company-specific success strategies and implementation designs that could help the line manager navigate and recalibrate where necessary. Similarly, Human Resources can report up emerging and unique issues that might need senior management attention.

If miscommunication is the issue, some of it might be attributed to generational differences: the manager with longer service being more adherent to "the way we've always done things," while the newer worker, unencumbered by tradition, looks for ways to improve on past practices. Members of the technology-friendly "Generation Y" (born between 1978 and 1990) bring instant messaging and other handheld information gathering tools to the workplace in direct contrast to written memos and circulars. There is bound to be tension and miscommunication. However, those who have given Generation Y some latitude in carrying out their duties have found that this tech-friendly age group is willing to try new things, as they often look at things a little differently.[14]

If generational or communications differences do not account for the lax approach toward diversity and inclusion, the gap could be attributed directly to a lack of understanding of the relevance of such an initiative in their daily work lives. According to researcher and author Yoji Cole,

> "Too often, diversity initiatives receive full support from the chief executive, a yeoman's effort from human resources, and the undivided focus of the diversity department, but they stall when they hit middle or line managers, who don't understand the relevance to their daily activities and goals."[15]

While there was no one, perfect plan for motivating the middle manager, there were five general themes that emerged from Cole's review of industry leaders in diversity.

1. Include middle management from the start. Middle managers must hear from the C-suite that inclusion and diversity are the aspirations of the company, not from the EEO/AA manager or diversity director.
2. Use employee-resource groups and surveys. They make a difference. The results of surveys and feedback from resource groups help middle managers stay focused, and ensure fairness.
3. Make diversity training mandatory for middle managers.
4. Include diversity metrics in performance appraisals.
5. Link successful accomplishment of diversity goals to middle manager compensation.

A CEO once observed during the course of an audit that his job was "not to change attitudes," but rather to "control behaviors." Some managers might not innately believe that diversity is relevant to their daily activities, but if senior leaders evaluate them on their diversity performance, recognize them for their results, and consistently remind them of its importance to the organization, their actions will supersede any attitudinal reservations they might possess.

Bottoms-Up Communications

There are innumerable ways to receive upward communications from the rank-and-file employee. E-mail has become the new "suggestion box." From the suggestion box to employee surveys and focus groups, employers attempt to identify where there might be poor morale, risk management issues, waste, fraud, and abuse. For some, it is management's open-door policy that brings forth the best communications. Not only does an open-door policy assist in bringing forth suggestions, but it can also assist in airing grievances and concerns. Care should be taken when establishing such a policy. Management must seriously and carefully consider suggestions brought forward or risk being accused of "management's phony attempts at caring for its employees."[16] Likewise, management must listen to the messengers — not discount them. If there is the belief, feeling, or conjecture that management is defensive or critical when suggestions are made, the suggestions will cease. Unfortunately, if systemic issues exist, they will surface through other potentially more costly outlets, such as the formal employee grievance process. HR professionals can avert costly and harmful employment disputes by ensuring that management supports the programs in place in an active, timely, and relevant manner.

Employee Input: Accepted or Rejected?

There are some who feel that the workplace no longer values their thoughts or input. With the ever-changing world of work continuously undergoing twists and turns, employers are forced to meet skills demands and economic cycles in a variety of ways — from workforce expansion to workforce contraction and from decreased use of permanent workers to increased use of temporary, contingent, contract, or independent workers. The mix varies depending on the industry, but one thing is certain: the lines that distinguished one type of employee from another have been permanently blurred, as talent gets tapped from different sources in pursuit of common objectives. The use of consultants has increased, be it to assist with recruitment, redefine business strategies, or recommend a new marketing campaign. Consulting services run the gamut — from the strategic to the tactical — and cover every activity a company might undertake.

Meanwhile, both the rank-and-file employees and internal managers have had to cede some of their influence to these outside sources in part because consultants are seen as offering a broader, less insular perspective to issues, and in part also to protect themselves against any potential fallout, should the counsel offered backfire. Such consultants could indeed have overarching industrial knowledge vital to moving the company forward, or they could simply transfer practices from one workplace to another. It is not unusual for management consultants to listen to the employee base (whether it is direct conversation or survey results), process their views and concerns, repackage their advice, and present it to the executive team. Listening to the employee — not simply hearing but truly listening — might in fact present the insight and solution that the company seeks.

A Case in Point

Jon is an HR professional, assigned to a business unit. As such, he has a direct reporting relationship to line management, but also reports on a dotted line to corporate Human Resources. As part of an efficiency study, consultants were hired to ensure Human Resources had the tools it needed to be effective in this matrix management arrangement. Upon learning of the consultants' observations, Jon stated: "I've sent memos to senior management stating the same recommendations you are making today. I've got a drawer full! Mine never got traction. I'm glad they're listening to you. I'll help point you in the right direction."

There are workplace settings where policy changes and conforming HR practices are seen by line managers and employees alike as riding on the coattails of a recently published book, or an offsite conference, or of some nugget learned at an executive development course. There is a tendency to adopt a practice when others tout its results. While ideas can abound from employees, it is the "what's working at my competitor" that tends to get attention, regardless of differences in management style, size of workforce, or other uniqueness. Employees know what is going on. They want to be heard and valued. Lend them an ear. It might not be easy, but it is valuable to the success of the organization. HR professionals are uniquely positioned to ensure the free flow of communications and input from all types of employees and sources. Sandwiched between corporate HR and the operating business line, the HR professional serves as the link, the problem solver, the navigator, and often the voice of reason. Our experience has shown time and time again that HR professionals have a deep understanding not only of the people management issues but also of the operational challenges involved.

Harking back to Johnson & Johnson's Credo (see Chapter 1), employees must feel free to make suggestions and complaints. With today's global marketplace driving rapid shifts and realignments, being open and receptive to ideas and input can only strengthen workplace relationships.

Communicating Within: Open the Lines of Communication

For the goal of diversity to be met at all levels and throughout all practices, communications must be open in all directions and a variety of channels must be utilized. While surveys and focus groups elicit valuable feedback, many advocate simple conversations as the best way to give and receive input. Yet, if the employee senses resistance to his/her observations, a roadblock to open communications or a lost opportunity to obtain valuable information might ensue. Sensitivity to the communications process will engender trust, leading to a more cohesive, harmonious and productive work environment.

Confidential Communications

Every company possesses privileged or confidential information that, if revealed, could cause competitive harm or economic disadvantage. For example, staffing levels that precipitously fall or rise in a division could signal a strategic business change that a company is preparing to make but not yet ready to disclose. Similarly, nondisclosure severance agreements between employees and the employer — often utilized at voluntary or involuntary termination — allow the employer to settle disputes without costly court battles or defense costs. Discussions within the C-suite on strategic planning, plant closings, acquisitions, or impending layoffs are other areas warranting confidentiality. There could also be a privacy concern restricting those in Human Resources from having full access to all employee data. For example, the person developing and monitoring the salary administration system might have no knowledge of, or oversight of the executive compensation system or benefits administration. The laws require that all HR systems be administered in a nondiscriminatory fashion. Heartfelt leaders understand this and go beyond the requirements of the law by insisting on coordination and cooperation across functions in order to gain employee confidence and satisfaction. Who will do the monitoring? Who is part of those discussions? These answers will vary from employer to employer, but HR professionals are the link between the line manager and his/her employment decisions and the results of those actions.

Communications are Key

Communications are key to the successful implementation of any strategic plan — diversity efforts are no different. If an employer feels the need for realignment or repositioning, it is important to ask the employees for their input rather than following the trend or path laid out by others. What works in one company might not work in another. This can be clearly seen with the introduction of broadbanding of salaries in companies that are so hierarchical and rigid that the implementation of such was doomed before the ink dried.

Similarly, how one company attracts and obtains diverse talent might not yield the same success at another company due to geographic differences, management styles, and type of business. Employees are closer to the product and the problems. Their observations and advice are dynamic. Whether the issue is a division not receptive to diversity efforts; managers using the discretion in the compensation structure to favor one group over another; or, the inordinate placement of women and people of color in certain traditional roles, communications down, up and within are vital to success. For the CEO committed to development and retention of a diverse workforce, speaking from the heart about that commitment via a host of media is critical to ensuring buy-in and confidence from the rank-and-file. Communications should be used as motivational tools and recognition of successes, as well as for the conveyance of information and expectations. For the HR professional, charged with interfacing both with the C-suite and the line manager, communicating the desires of the C-suite while encouraging line management's ownership of the process and its results is the challenge. That diversity challenge begins with, "Where are you looking for workers?" "Who is being recruited?" "Who is being hired?" "Where are they being placed?"

04 Find It in Your Heart: Recruiting and Hiring

"One would think that our universities would be leading the way in progressive thinking. You wouldn't think that in 2009 it would be more likely for an African American to become president of the United States than to be hired as head coach of a top-20 football program. But that seems to be the case." — Tony Dungy[1]

Heartfelt Leader

A Silicon Valley CEO, finding himself widowed with young children, came to realize very quickly the challenges that working parents face in balancing work and family responsibilities. Acting upon that newfound empathy and appreciation, he established one of the first company-sponsored day care centers and learning facilities in the nation. *Profound personal change can often trigger cultural transformation. Empathy coupled with action can produce progress.*

Recruit. E-cruit. Screen. Select.

Diversity of views, variances in opinions and experiences, different languages and backgrounds, and a variety of influences can all lead to expanding markets, better work products, improved quality of service, and greater profitability. How does the committed employer get there? Communicating the desire and the vision, consistently and persistently, needs to be aligned with commitment in action. The HR professional is the link between the desire and reality, between *ganas* and actually generating a diverse pool of applicants for consideration when making a selection.

A reserved, if not passive, CEO meets with his senior management team on an annual basis, and together they discuss diversity training needs as well as set diversity placement goals by division and product line, and across management levels. On an annual basis, as part of their performance management review, the CEO asks them to discuss how they are doing toward meeting their placement goals. Each year he hears the same feedback, "I had a Hispanic financial analyst who was going to come to us, but Company Y got her" or "We're just in a bedroom community where people of color don't want to live. They like living in cities. I can get them to come for an interview, but then they find there aren't many minorities in the town and decide they don't want to be so isolated" or "I'd love to hire a female civil engineer, but they drop out of engineering and go into computer sciences. All of our competitors will tell you the same thing." The list of explanations goes on and on. Each year, the CEO just shakes his head in an understanding way and tells the C-suite to just keep trying — the old worn-out, "better luck next year," conclusion to the diversity portion of the year-end discussion. An actively engaged CEO, firmly committed to diversity and inclusion, would think strategically, host diversity discussions frequently, hold the C-suite accountable for leveraged results, and understand that diversity is more than who has been hired. A comprehensive diversity strategy encompasses training, development, mentoring, and a myriad of other formal and informal practices to ensure that when people of diverse backgrounds are recruited they become successfully integrated into the workforce.

There are certainly employers who have made good faith efforts to hire women or professionals of color, only to lose them to a more lucrative hiring offer, a more culturally diverse city, or an industry with more desirable working conditions. When recruiting only a few diverse candidates out of a large group, their particular life situations may become more distinguishable and easier to recall. These same employers may not remember as readily, for example, the white male who went to a competitor, took a position in a different city, or stated that the culture was not a good fit. The natural tendency is to remember the few, the exceptions, rather than the norm.

The motivated leader does not focus down on the numbers — the one who declined an offer or the two who left the company — but focuses up and thinks strategically, asking: What's it going to take to make us an employer that is so welcoming of diversity and inclusion that we naturally attract diverse talent? What's it going to take to foster inclusion so that we don't keep losing our top talent? What can we do as leaders and employers in this community to make it a more welcoming community for people of different races and ethnicities?

A *Ganas*-led Leader
- » Explores all available sources of recruitment to broaden diversity;
- » Expects hiring efforts to foster a balanced workforce; and
- » Elevates others through inclusive staffing decisions.

Bringing the senior management team together, the inspired leader discusses the obstacles to that goal to determine whether the obstacles are educational, geographic, or cultural, and empowers the team to take ownership of solutions. Of vital importance is the role of Human Resources. As a strategic partner in these discussions, Human Resources can share successful strategies and offer feedback from employee surveys, recruitment efforts, exit interviews, and anecdotal information. HR professionals understand that there will always be peer companies with larger budgets for hiring, better benefits, or more attractive locations. Obstacles notwithstanding, they can effectively and successfully assist the company in overcoming such challenges. If they are sincere in their commitment, they will look into their heart for answers to some difficult questions: What can we do to make sure the next hire has a soft landing, a mentor, and a better experience? Where can we identify, recruit, and hire employees who want to be a part of something innovative, to make a difference? How and where can we change to foster an inclusive, participatory, engaged workforce? What other value-added experiences and exposures can we offer? "The first thing I ask a good candidate is what they want to achieve in the next few years. Good people always want to build something, and be a part of something."[2] If Human Resources is excluded from these conversations and their role is relegated to that of process — posting positions, following paperwork, chasing staffing files — a vital link between inspired motivation and action is broken.

Unfortunately, a recent survey reports that two out of five corporate management teams still do not view Human Resources as a strategic partner, thereby losing out on the benefits of engaging such expertise. However, among the largest employers (50,000 employees or more), the role of Human Resources is now considered critically important by over 70 percent of those surveyed.[3] Whatever the impetus — financial profit, a talent war, growing skills gap, or global competition — forging a strategic alliance with Human Resources is a partnership that elevates performance and effectively advances the mission and objectives of a company.

A Goal Without a Plan Is Just a Wish[4]

With the backing and visible support of the C-suite leadership, HR managers must encourage, engage, and enable the hiring manager to think and act strategically when recruiting and hiring. Rather than resorting to business as usual, or "this is how we always get workers," each of the hiring manager's individual placements must be seen as part of a whole. What if everyone took a pass on diversity and hired from a homogenous pool? What if everyone's outreach was hampered by remembrances of diversity "failures" of the past ... perhaps an individual who left the company, or never returned from maternity leave, or who didn't perform? What if everyone chose to overlook resumes in which the applicant had an ethnic sounding name or a last name difficult to pronounce? Every action and decision will have a cumulative effect on the results. Most important, attaching such attitudinal biases to the selection process will render the outcome incomplete, inefficient, and wasteful of human talent. The HR professional can serve as the link between commitment and action. How? By working through stereotypical barriers with line managers; debunking false assumptions and preconceived notions; pointing out success stories; discussing how diverse talent can create new market opportunities; and presenting highly accomplished and qualified candidates, without regard to race, gender, ethnicity, or any other personal characteristic. With the encouragement and assistance of Human Resources, line managers can redesign their outreach efforts, balance their employment patterns, and create a culture of inclusion and workplace fairness. In the process, the line manager fulfills the expectations of the heartfelt leader, one action at a time.

Follow the Leader

Benjamin Franklin is reputed to have coined the saying, "Well done is better than well said." A rallying cry for inclusion must be followed by action if the C-suite is to have any credibility within its workforce and community. Diversity at the highest levels of management is the most obvious example of CEO commitment in action. Many organizations track and report on corporate board representations as a sign of commitment to diversity. But for these individuals to have reached such a level, they had to have been part of a pipeline of executive talent, whether the pipeline came out of the public sector, academia, corporate America, or nonprofit organizations. It is this level of executive talent that ultimately populates corporate boards. Absent such talent, boards will continue to be devoid of diversity. Diversity at the senior management ranks, however, is pivotal to the final and complete integration of talent at all levels of leadership. Reaching this level of diversity requires significant effort, active leadership, and a passion for *ganas* — inspired inclusion.

Every new hire, every promotion, and every rotational assignment in upper management is a visible sign of the C-suite's commitment — or not. Most companies will look internally for talent before going outside. Many report having an average internal promotion rate of between 70 percent to 90 percent. In these cases, staffing practices, executive talent development, and succession planning are critical efforts. For those companies whose practices allow for an infusion of talent at the highest levels, each external hire offers a unique opportunity to bring in diverse talent.

On the other hand, when these ranks remain homogenous and every opening is void of diverse candidates, it can bring into question the seriousness and sincerity of the commitment. "It's not a pipeline issue, it's an emotional issue. It's about the willingness of people to change. A lot of lip service is being paid ... but in order to thrive, organizations must fully engage every employee and fully serve every consumer."[5] It is below the C-suite that succession planning, talent development, and senior staffing systems come together. It is also at this intersection where systems can go awry if the people guiding those systems are not working in concert and united in purpose. The HR professional can help facilitate a cohesive process of staffing, planning, and development when involved in the action. Many, many instances have been reported where a hiring executive extended an offer or created a new position without the knowledge or involvement of Human Resources. The HR manager became involved after the fact — verifying immigration status, completing application forms, and processing the new hire after he or she reported for work. This is a missed opportunity. When Human Resources is not actively involved, good faith efforts to include talented professionals of color and women could be overlooked, biased placement patterns might emerge, and salary inequities might result.

The committed leader must make sure that oversight and accountability begins with the senior staff. At every point in the process the questions must be asked:

1. Does this pool contain qualified applicants from diverse populations?
2. Has the sourcing agent ensured they have sincerely attempted such? If so, how?
3. Are there exit points in the process?
   a. Do diverse candidates fall out at the interview phase?
   b. Do diverse candidates fall out after a review of external assessment center results?
   c. Are there other screens in the process?

A Case for Not Following the Leader

Just as a new CEO can change the culture of a company with inspired leadership resulting in diversity at the highest levels, the opposite is also possible. A new CEO can undo the diversity efforts of the past much faster than the time (years) it took to reach that level of participation.

A Case in Point

"We were doing so well with our diversity efforts until our new CEO came onboard. While he says he's committed to diversity, the women and people of color at the VP level and above disappeared almost overnight. There are no black secretaries in the C-suite either. He's brought in an all-Caucasian support staff from his last company. If you can't find diversity in the clerical ranks, how can we believe he wants diversity in the management ranks?" — *Fortune* 1000 diversity manager

---

When the new CEO is a person of color or a woman, the expectations are higher and their actions are scrutinized even more closely on all fronts. The male and white employees might wonder whether they will be treated fairly and given ample opportunities, while the diverse employee base might expect greater emphasis on diversity efforts with faster progress. Inspired leaders who are women or people of color have additional responsibilities by virtue of their rare ascent to the top. "Some women fail, just like some men fail, but their failure is pronounced because there are few women in management positions."[6] Their actions are scrutinized and magnified and often carry repercussions beyond the individual, to the ethnic, racial, or gender group they represent. Such visibility and exposure can create greater sensitivity to ensure that their decisions and actions are balanced — not leaning in any particular direction. The heartfelt leader understands this responsibility and the need for transparency, accountability, and integrity in all processes and decision-making.

Below the C-suite, in the under-suites, the processes for hiring tend to be more formal and systematized. Yet, even with programs and policies in place, it is the actual practices that can undermine the integrity of the system if not closely monitored and evaluated. Creating a variety of hiring sources and outreach efforts is the first step toward developing a diverse pool of candidates.

Fish Where the Fish Are

When Elizabeth Dole became Secretary of Labor and was recruiting for talent to join her team, she directed her staff to "cast the net far and wide." Outreach and recruitment efforts are the portal for most new hires, especially at the entry professional levels. Word-of-mouth networks also provide a pipeline of talent. It is the HR professional's responsibility to develop a broad recruitment strategy, one that taps into diverse networks and contacts. Taking that responsibility seriously, Human Resources must make certain that their networks are current, dynamic, and representative of the rich and diverse talent that exists. Professional associations, often with branches that are race-, ethnicity-, or gender-specific, serve as excellent sources for expanding the pool of talent. Historically, many companies satisfied their legal affirmative action obligations by setting goals and hiring at the entry levels through special interest networks or local community organizations, while leaving intact their associations for upper level hires that mostly did not yield diverse slates of candidates. This practice significantly delayed the full integration of talent at all levels and areas of employment. Even with the legal tagline on all advertisements and publications affirming that they were an EEO/ AA employer, many continued on, business as usual, and did not change their hiring sources or processes.

Years ago there may have also been some validity to the statements that there were no women or people of color in entire fields, lines of work, or disciplines. Occupational and industry gaps still exist, but, more often than not, the lack of diversity in recruitment and hiring is due to limited outreach efforts, lack of follow through, and the desire to skip steps and fill the job as quickly as possible, often depriving the company of valuable sources and talent. The *ganas* for an inclusive workforce takes a different approach.

The motivated employer understands that simple statements such as "I just can't find any" will not lead to the desired results. While this might be a valid answer, the inspired leader will work to cultivate relationships with diverse sources, and develop a next generation of workers through college and university partnerships, in short, to prime the pump. Inspired leaders understand that there must be accountability and safeguards built into the hiring process to ensure integrity. The HR role is essential for assisting the hiring manager with outreach to nontraditional sources of talent. Corporate staffing must ensure that the hiring manager is involved in the process from the start and committed to successful recruitment, staffing, and placement. *Ganas* for inclusion — aligning the expectation with the implementation — bolsters the chances to forge a partnership with a common goal, check points, and a strategy for success.

Within the workforce of a very traditional male industry lies a clustering of minorities and women in one business unit, which prompted a discussion with the line manager. "Other managers will stop by and ask me the same thing. I tell them it didn't happen overnight. I had to work with each employee and their particular situation. I had three part-timers who were very good workers. Over the years, I worked with Human Resources to get them promoted, which was not easy to do because it was against our culture. When their particular circumstances changed and they went to full-time, I had a very talented and loyal group. Another woman was a secretary in whom I saw not only great potential, but also an interest in advancement. I encouraged her to take some courses, which helped move her into the professional ranks. A few of my summer interns who are women and minorities have now moved on to other units. The one thing they all have in common is that they continued to take on challenging opportunities and wanted to expand. It's all about knowing and growing your talent pool."[7]

Diversity efforts embrace not only hiring targets but also combining such efforts with mentoring, coaching, training, and communications to ensure that the new employee understands the culture and expectations. Managers are encouraged to not be singularly focused on checking a hiring box goal, but rather on ensuring that there are a host of entry points for new talent and a support system in place for a successful arrival and integration. *Ganas* inspires the employer and staffing team to look beyond the perceived or real need for one of these or a few of those, to questions such as:

»   Where and how can I find and meet the best and brightest?

»   What do we offer as an employer to attract such talent?

»   What other sources can broaden the pool of prospects for consideration?

»   Are there other colleges and universities with whom we might develop a relationship for future interns and graduates?

»   Why do we turn over our diverse talent so frequently? With the costs to replace an employee ranging from 100 percent to 150 percent of the employee's salary, where are the exit points, and why?

Similarly, what good is a commitment to diversity if there is not a similar commitment to inclusion — to accepting, valuing, and engaging everyone — so that everyone has an opportunity to thrive? The honest, genuine *ganas* for an inclusive, empowered workforce is not simply a paradigm shift, but a new way of thinking, of acting, and of doing business altogether. For many, that new way of doing business begins with developing a future work force.

Priming the Pump

Gone are the days when employers could drop into a college or graduate school recruitment fair and swoop up the top talent. Employers looking for that one-off recruitment effort without a sustained relationship have come up empty-handed. On the other hand, employers who have developed ongoing relationships via co-op arrangements, internships, part-time employment, and the like, have found college, university, and graduate school recruitment efforts extremely beneficial. *The Employer's Guide to College Recruiting and Hiring*[8] stresses that committed employers ought to target schools based on specific needs and areas; develop effective strategies for sourcing, recruiting, and retaining candidates; establish contacts on campus; position their organization as an employer of choice; and, invigorate their diversity recruitment efforts.

Historically black colleges and universities have been a traditional source of diverse talent. Yet, corporate recruiters might overlook these sources in favor of "alumni" schools, more "prestigious" universities, or their preferred schools. "We have core schools for recruiting, and we only recruit actively at those core schools. For each school, we have a set number of offers that we make based on interviews. On average, we make 10 offers from each school. We also review other applications received online, and we do hire from this pool as well — but generally those decisions are made after we interview on campus."[9] Recruiters, unable to financially compete with others for the scarce diversity at such prestigious institutions, simply give up — case closed — and report back to corporate that while they tried they could not compete with those employers with deeper pockets. The *ganas* for diversity is not very strong in these situations. For the committed employer, not only does establishing a relationship with historically black colleges and universities bear fruit, so too does giving local youth inspiration and hope, by developing a stable relationship with a neighboring high school, college or university that can turn into a strong partnership for producing a future workforce.

While it is easy to blame those in staffing and recruiting for not bringing broad diversity to the candidate pool, some proffer that the recruiter is only presenting hat the employer actually wants. As some recruiters' performance is evaluated based upon referrals turned into hires, they only surface those candidates whom they believe reflect the corporate image. In these situations they reportedly receive an "unspoken profile" of what the hiring managers wanted from recruits — the corporate fit factor.[10] Understanding this subtle form of bias exists with some employers and their recruitment agents, college and university placement offices track the success rates of their graduates both in terms of initial job placements and starting salaries. When there appears to be steering of a gender or race into certain entry-level positions, or large differentials in starting salaries, academics have challenged such practices. University placement offices work to ensure their partnerships are with employers possessing *ganas* for an inclusive, fair workplace that operates with integrity. In many industries and professions — for example, book publishing — the line manager is often plugged into the potential labor market and as such is in a position to guide the recruiting team. The employer motivated beyond legal compliance and the immediate bottom line understands that lack of skills is the biggest impediment to full inclusion of diverse talent. High schools are the pipeline into higher education and vocational occupations. Mentoring at this level has been proven an effective method to stem the dropout rate, primarily affecting diverse populations in the United States.[11]

> "I was inspired by the mere success of my mentor; the shared experiences about her road to success was a guiding light which motivated me and helped me understand that many before me struggled and achieved." — High school mentee

Moved by their *ganas*, some employers have partnered with others to build consortiums and other affiliations for at-risk youth. Whether it is support of the Youth Automotive Training Center (Deerfield Beach, Florida) or support of at-risk youths in the arts, ministry, or the semiconductor industry, like-minded leaders come together to address the needs of those who need a hand-up not a handout.

High school, college, and university relationships based upon mentoring, internships, career shadowing, and part-time work are effective methods of priming the pump for a stable and diverse future workforce while providing hope and inspiration needed during students' formal educational years.

Relationships with neighboring schools are a strong method of acquiring future workers. With the birth of the Internet in 1990, employers' future talent base expanded exponentially. America's present and future workers are plugged-in and tech savvy. The Internet is their playground. From online search and referral agencies to video resumes, the Internet is a powerful tool to foster diversity.

Work the Net

Some say that we will begin to refer to historical events as pre-Internet and post-Internet much as we refer to history in terms of B.C. and A.D. This is the case in recruitment and hiring. Today's workforce is the most connected, networked society of employees that has ever existed. There are multiple search engines changing the manner in which employees are identified, interviewed and hired. It is not uncommon for employers to post positions on Jobster.com, Yahoo! HotJobs, Job.com, CareerBuilder.com, or Monster.com when going outside the company for talent. Similarly, employees post resumes on these and other websites. Networking frameworks such as LinkedIn, Facebook, and MySpace offer avenues for individuals to connect and conduct business. Twenty-somethings rely on the Internet as a way to socialize and communicate, as well as look for employment options. It is even becoming more common for a recruiter to receive unsolicited video resumes. Some even predict that it will not be long before individuals start selling their skills and expertise to the highest bidder on eBay.

While some rigor is encouraged in all employment practices to ensure nondiscrimination, the traditional lines that define an applicant are becoming more and more blurred as employers search the Internet using the various websites and hold on to resumes of impressive talent. For example, Deloitte LLP received 316,000 resumes of candidates applying for experienced professional openings in 2008. While 21,000 made the first cut through a telephone screen, and 11,000 were called in for interviews, those who did not get job offers remain in the database for future reference, according to the company.[12]

Though the touch of the keyboard brings a host of potential employment candidates to the screen, emerging legal and moral issues include:

» Does an employer need to list or track the entire batch of Internet resumes or video resumes reviewed?

» At what point does a video resume or weblink become an "applicant" requiring tracking to ensure nondiscrimination in hiring or screening?

» Is this source of candidates discriminatory against the blind or visually impaired?

The federal government issued specific guidelines in 2006 for defining an Internet applicant for those who hold federal contracts or subcontracts.[13] That definition will once again be open to revision in the near future. Rather than relying on the existing or revised guidance, the heartfelt leader motivated by inclusion will ensure that there are documented, neutral criteria for reviewing resumes and applications and that there is accountability to ensure consistent application in practice. Most important, regardless of the process used, the *ganas*-practicing leader will insist on diversity as an expected outcome.

Ad Hoc Networks

No matter how sincere the heartfelt leader, there will almost always be instances when outside hiring occurs without the direct oversight of Human Resources. These hires tend to be at the more senior levels, and the hire tends to fall outside the formal processes of the HR applicant systems. When queried as to the hire's origin, more often than not a senior executive learned of this candidate through a colleague; personally knew of the individual; was sent a resume with an endorsement by a respected professional; or noticed this individual at an event, a presentation, or from a previous interview. He or she just put the person's resume in their bottom drawer — a little cache for future use. Oftentimes, the executive is tempted to believe that the individual is "uniquely qualified" or possesses singular skills nonexistent in other potential candidates. In these situations, the sense of urgency to hire the individual before someone else does trumps all the systems and procedures in place. The action is rationalized by assurances that this is an "exception to the rule." Without checks and balances, exceptions to the rule can become the norm, as few wish to lose immediacy and control to a potentially more lengthy and unpredictable hiring process.

Ensuring diversity considerations as well as preventing unlawful discrimination is more difficult when such ad hoc systems are allowed to function. The heartfelt leader works to ensure that all in the C-suite understand the strength of the commitment to diversity and utilizes a performance plan with accountability measures to ensure that all understand that commitment to diversity and that legal equal opportunity in employment is not one person's job or one office's mission, but must be at the root of all personnel activities and practices. Establishing and reiterating that shared vision, coupled with joint responsibility for goal attainment, will assist in making the vision a reality.

Employee Referrals

It is understandable and laudable that a heartfelt leader, proud of the competence and quality of the company's workforce, would want to attract more of the same. Employee referral systems, in which employees are not only able to refer others but encouraged to do so (often with a stipend or bonus for referrals-turned-hires) are one way to expand a company's talent base. "Employee referrals aren't just a good source of quality hires — they are the No. 1 source of high-quality hires,"[14] with at least one employer reporting that 50 percent of new hires coming through employee referrals and another reporting a $2,500 referral-hire bonus.[15] Utilizing an automated employee referral system that is easy to use, is readily available and provides feedback to the referrer adds to the efficiency of the system. Targeting high-performing employees for referrals is part of the recruitment strategy at some companies. "Good people refer good people."[16]

Employee referrals serve as the preferred source of recruitment for many employers. However, these programs might not yield a wide enough pool of diverse talent, especially if the referrals are coming from a non-diverse population of workers. The inspired leader, attuned to this possibility, will empower the HR manager to supplement this practice with other processes should the employee referral system yield a homogenous pool of candidates. Similarly, Human Resources must monitor each step of the process just as any other form of recruitment, from referrals to hires, to ensure an inclusive outcome.

Temp to Permanent Transitions

One method of viewing talent before making a permanent hiring offer is through the use of temporary staffing services. The use of these services has increased dramatically in recent years, as companies in cyclical industries and others not wanting to add to their permanent employment base for various reasons opt for this approach. The growing ranks of temporary staffing services include the placement of professionals in the finance, information technology, and engineering fields. Some firms specialize in health care placements; others exclusively place lawyers. "[L]aw firms are learning that they can save money and test potential employees by hiring them on a temporary basis, then transferring them to regular full-time basis."[17] Some state that the "temp-to-perm model" is the best way to hire. While some are "permanent" temps wishing to stay on the temp rolls for the flexibility, others use the temporary placement route as a way to segue back into the workforce after a leave of absence. The same cautions that existed with the administrative, light industrial temps-to-hires of past years surface with professional placements as well — ensuring that there is no bias in the system that would disproportionately exclude diverse talent from selection.

Jeff Joerres is the CEO of Manpower, Inc., the third largest staffing services company in the world. He understands the critical importance of referring talent without regard to race, gender or ethnicity, and the competitive advantage of doing so.

> "At Manpower, diversity is directly tied to the DNA of the organization and the fundamental belief that there is a role for every individual in the world of work. Long before corporate diversity positions, diversity departments, and diversity suppliers, Manpower was finding the best in everyone and putting it to work. In fact, we were a pioneer in creating opportunities for women to engage and thrive in the workforce, beginning in 1948, when it was not yet socially acceptable for women to work outside of the home and develop careers. We also played an important role in providing jobs to people of color in the 1960s, a pivotal era for racial diversity within the United States. This commitment is at the core of what we do — connecting people with jobs, training, and tools that

enable them to support themselves and contribute to the community."[18]

Addressing the importance of having inclusive practices to attract and retain top talent Joerres observed,

> "Two trends are now reshaping the world of work: the growing dominance of the service sector and the shrinking working-age population. These two trends add up to a global talent crunch that will only get tighter, especially after we emerge from the current financial crisis. To address this problem, governments and enterprises must determine the best way to expand their workforces now. One way is to tap into labor and talent pools that are underrepresented, such as women. Barriers that can keep organizations from attracting and retaining such a vital talent pool largely have to do with inflexible work structures. One area that reflects the old way of thinking and discourages women from participating involves policies that deter women from returning to work. More than 93 percent of women in the U.S. who take a break from the workplace — usually to have children — want to return, but only 74 percent do so. Some reasons for this include protected maternity leave duration, the availability of part-time work, and the ability to work from home. True flexible work practices that address these concerns would be an important element to attract and retain talent."[19]

Joerres has been widely recognized as a heartfelt and innovative business leader. One of his hallmarks has been the drive for diversity within Manpower. Martha Artiles, Manpower's chief diversity officer, described Joerres's approach this way,

> "He understands the value and importance of fresh thinking that comes from engaged, diverse perspectives. He makes

clear and sets the expectations with his executive team that diversity is how the business must operate. This is embedded in key organizational frameworks such as the Strategic Execution Framework, which guides the company's strategy. He also integrates the message of inclusion in key communications vehicles, both internally and externally."[20]

Executive Search Firms

Employers often turn to executive search firms to find upper mid- and senior executive-level talent. Sometimes, the company has internal candidates it wants to compare against the talent available in the marketplace. Most of the time, there is no one identified internally as having the necessary skills or as "ready now," and the search is focused exclusively on external talent. In both instances, the search firm is retained and becomes responsible for the development, identification, assessment, and presentation of candidates. Once the company conducts the interviews and makes a final selection, the search firm gets involved again in compensation, perks, and benefits discussions and in resolving any other logistical or personal issues that may affect the placement.

Search firms are given broad latitude with which to do their work. And even though the processes used are fairly standard across the industry, there is considerable independence exercised by each search consultant. Like all other industries, some consultants have great sensitivity and commitment toward diversity, while others don't take the time or make the effort to nurture relationships in nontraditional networks that could render a more diverse slate of candidates. It takes longer to conduct a search with an emphasis on diversity, because so many potential candidates have left corporate America to start their own businesses or to enter a different economic sector. Also, it is often more difficult to engage diverse candidates because of past experiences. Many of these same individuals have felt used over the years. They question the sincerity of the effort and resist engagement. There is a wariness that the call from the firm may be just to satisfy the diversity obligation, just to be placed as the "diversity candidate" without any realistic chance of being seriously considered. This can be seen in forced pools in which women or minorities are required to be on the slate.

Search consultants influence the outcome of searches by the way they present and discuss candidates. Having a consultant with an active and visible commitment to diversity can create a level playing field for all the candidates. Heartfelt leaders will be served well by carefully choosing consultants, by managing the process, and by ensuring that the executive talent pool identified is, indeed, the result of a rigorous and thorough search effort.

"Is this an affirmative action search? Are you calling me just to put me on the list, or are you really serious?"
— A response to a search call from an individual of color

The Talent Tiff

Employers develop creative packages to attract talent that is in high demand. "It all comes down to understanding what the workers we need are looking for in their next job. Some people are looking to make money, and some are looking to make the future. Those aren't mutually exclusive, but they tell you a lot about what you can offer someone."[21] When talent is scarce and the competition stiff, employers end up paying a premium to attract the right candidates. The pay differential that develops between a new executive hire and one with long tenure can be sizeable. Such apparent inequities are not necessarily discriminatory, but can lead to compensation imbalances difficult to overcome, as well as morale problems affecting retention. Those who have been on the inside suspect the compensation variances and have a hard time accepting them, often triggering resentment and poor teamwork.

It is important that the heartfelt employer keep the vision on the goal — that of a cohesive, inclusive, and collaborative workforce. Human Resources can facilitate the achievement of such a goal by ensuring that the hiring decisions taken are fair and equitable; by communicating this message; and by coaching and assisting managers in providing honest feedback to those feeling undervalued. Individuals want to know where they stand in terms of opportunities and growth potential. Transparency and honesty in explaining choices made will not only clear the air but also provide an incentive to re-engage and drive performance. Whether the internal talent didn't possess the right mix of skills and experiences, whether recent performance had been lackluster; or whether additional development was required, Human Resources can pave the way for such discussions.

Monitor Hiring Processes and "Hiring Hoops"

Making sure that the hiring process is level and free of invisible barriers provides the first steps toward a welcoming workplace. Job postings that set out minimum qualification requirements and articulate an invitation for all to apply through a stated commitment to equal employment opportunities afford all applicants a level playing field. However, when the criteria expand to include more selective requirements, such as a taking an aptitude or skills test, background check, medical evaluation, drug screening, valid drivers' license or other documentation, keeping accurate records and monitoring the outcomes grow in importance to preserve a process free of bias.

At the highest corporate levels, the hiring process becomes more subjective. Additional interviews; detailed reference reports; and the use of external assessment centers to evaluate "corporate fit," "leadership skills," and "opportunities for further growth" are factored into the employment decision. The employer motivated by a heartfelt desire for diversity will monitor these processes to ensure that they are not selecting out diverse candidates due to tests, criteria, or endorsements more heavily favoring one group over another. Human Resources can provide the link that enables strategic hiring while ensuring an open and free flow of all available talent.

Unlawful Bias and Discrimination: Impediments to Diversity

Discrimination is costly in every sense of the word. Heartfelt leaders envision a workplace that transcends the regimented requirements of the law to a higher level of enrichment of ideas, creativity, and innovation through diverse thinking and perspectives. To reach that higher level of awareness, the state of the law and recent decisions can serve to inform and can provide an underpinning, yet not become the be-all and end-all. In relation to hiring:

» In 2005 the Equal Employment Opportunity Commission (EEOC) required a major trendy outfitter to pay $40 million in restitution to thousands of black, Latino, Asian, and other applicants and employees of color who were passed over for hire and promotion for biased and discriminatory reasons.[22] The agency found that individuals who did not possess the company's vision of the "all-American look" were denied opportunities.

» In 2007 the Office of Federal Contract Compliance Programs (OFCCP) of the U.S. Department of Labor reached a $275,000 settlement with a communications company engaged in gender discrimination. The agency found that 539 women applying for positions as financial-service and technical support representatives during a one-year period were systemically denied employment. In addition to the financial settlement on their behalf, the company agreed to hire 22 women and take immediate corrective measures to ensure nondiscrimination in hiring.[23]

In relation to initial job placement, route or product line:

» EEOC found that subtle racism occurred when the nation's largest drugstore used race as a factor in determining where to place black pharmacists, generally placing them in low-performing stores and in predominantly black communities.[24]

In relation to job descriptions and policies:

» In 2005, the EEOC resolved that a drive-through restaurant must pay back pay to female applicants who were denied food preparation positions because of their gender and revise its job descriptions and employee handbook and policies to make them gender-neutral.[25]

And, in relation to search and referral agency staffing:

» In 2009 a national staffing agency was ordered to place applicants for employment without regard to gender and to pay a financial settlement of $250,000. The staffing agency was found to have restricted women to a narrow set of jobs and abided to client requests for men only when staffing positions. "This settlement is a stark reminder to businesses: A customer's preference to be staffed or served only by workers of a particular gender is never an excuse to engage in illegal sex discrimination," stated the EEOC acting chairman.[26]

» In 2008, the EEOC found that a referral agency in Indianapolis not only failed to refer black applicants and those over 40 for assignments but also unlawfully retaliated against employees who objected to these referral policies.[27]

Recruitment Rewards

Diversity efforts are continually challenged to prove their worth in the workplace. In economically challenging times, the culture of return on investment (ROI) reigns supreme. HR professionals work to quantify and measure, validate and convince. The general tenets that diversity yields better products serving a diverse customer base, produces greater job satisfaction, and can improve efficiency are predicated upon diversity in recruitment and hiring as the threshold. If America's diversity is left untapped, we will never know how great we can actually be.

The Key: A Comprehensive and Cohesive Approach

Every employer must make strategic decisions on how best to identify and tap into our nation's diverse talent pool. There is no one "best" strategy to recruiting and hiring a highly qualified, energized, diverse workforce. But, rather, each employer working with Human Resources must make strategic alliances with organizations, colleges and universities, and professional groups to prime the pump for future workers. A review of all hiring practices and the resultant talent pool will steer the employer motivated by the goal of diversity to avenues requiring balance or refinement. Recruitment practices vary by level and by manager in many workplaces, and, no matter how committed the C-suite is to diversity — even embracing policies to promote such — it is the practices that may appear at odds with that goal.

Hiring decisions are not uniform in practice. Ten new financial analysts may be hired, but their titles may vary, as well as the terms of their compensation and organizational assignment. These decisions result in compensation differentials, business/line assignments with greater/lesser budgets and financial goals, as well as level of responsibility (see Figure 4.1). A comprehensive, cohesive approach to outreach and hiring will ensure that all of these entry factors are free from bias and discrimination.

Hiring practices that bring forth diverse talent for consideration must be fostered over those practices that do not. Similarly, managers must not be protective of their successful hiring and the diversity they acquire, especially when sharing the talent across business units or property lines will serve to develop the employee. Instead, the managers who not only hire but also cross-fertilize their diverse talent pool must be rewarded for sharing their success. It is the totality of management's hiring decisions that will lead to that inclusive, diverse workforce. Just as "a rising tide lifts all boats," so too will the diversity of the entire workplace be increased when individual managers' hiring decisions are leveraged. Such efforts may fall flat, however, if the workplace is neither conducive to, nor supportive of, opportunities for all, regardless of personal characteristics. Similarly, at mid- and upper-levels of the workforce, recruitment efforts must cover a broad spectrum of sources.

Figure 4.1

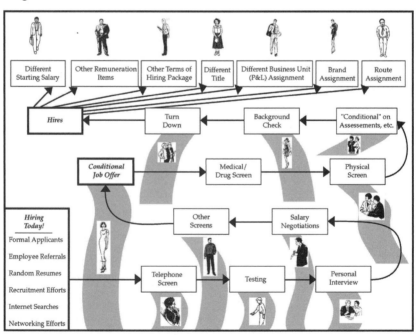

Periodic random sampling of position statements or job descriptions will assist in ensuring that these are free from gender-biased language. Reviews of applicant data and results to ensure nondiscrimination in hiring will ensure that outside vs. inside bias issues do not arise and that steering concerns or pay disparities do not surface later.

To move from numbers counting to "what's it going to take to be an employer of choice?," employers must include all levels of management in a comprehensive and cohesive strategy. Much like a tightly woven fabric, each manager's hiring decision provides the thread that must support the next and add to the overall pattern of the material. The day when a singular manager could boast that he or she recruited diverse talent successfully without any concern for other managers' or divisions' successes are quickly coming to an end. For it is the totality of the decisions that matters, as cross-fertilization and development will realign talent over time.

While diversity of applicants and workforce entrants are critical to fostering a diverse and inclusive workforce, placement patterns, initial salaries, and job positions and titles are also critical aspects of onboarding. Heartfelt leaders understand that if new hires are the seedlings, unbiased initial job placements; equity in title and position; and justifiable, consistent salary differentials at time of hire are the roots. Anything short of this will not only thwart growth and future development but also undermine the sincerity of the intention.

05 Put Heart into Developing Talent and Building Credentials

""If you have the will and the drive to grow in this organization, there is no ceiling for what you can achieve … McDonald's welcomes diversity of thought, experience, and expertise, and if you have the right combination of these attributes, you can realize tremendous success both personally and professionally." — Karen King[1]

Heartfelt Leader

At a consultation, the CEO was lamenting the fact that while he would love to provide women the opportunity for growth and advancement through international assignments, it was very difficult to find women who would uproot their families and relocate. While taking credit for a successful placement of a woman a few years back to an oversees position as her husband was a writer and could work anywhere he had Internet connectivity, he and a fellow executive commented that there was a brilliant candidate perfect for relocation, but her husband was a very notable attorney in town. When queried, "Have you asked her whether she would consider a global relocation?" there was an "aha moment" around the table as no one had asked her directly, but had made assumptions because of their knowledge of her husband's career. *Removing assumptions can yield surprising responses.*

Pipeline. Planning. Potential.

There is a certain flow to the cycle of work and advancement. First, the responsibility falls on the individuals to acquire the educational preparation and demonstrate the skill set that will get them hired. The burden falls squarely on the individuals to possess the knowledge, ability, and personal qualities that will make them desirable candidates for employment. Over time, with experience gained through the successful completion of various assignments and on-the-job training, the individuals will attract the attention of senior management. They get noticed, and soon the company takes an active interest in their retention. They begin to be included in the company's plans for development and succession. They are given more "face time" with upper management, and get invited to make high-level presentations and attend social activities with the executive team. They are assigned to high-profile task forces and initiatives, and selected to rotate through different functions and areas of responsibilities. Building a pipeline of talent — building "bench strength" — has become a corporate imperative in our highly competitive global environment.

As employees become more marketable, the company, which by now has invested significantly in their professional growth and development, becomes possessive and protective of them — their talent resources. At this stage in the cycle, the responsibility shifts and falls more heavily on the employer to produce opportunities that will motivate these high-performing individuals and keep them engaged. "These individuals are now corporate property, and we will do everything we can to keep them,"[2] expressed an executive vice president. The success of management in ensuring that everyone is given an opportunity to become "corporate property" will depend on the actions and decisions that it takes during the trajectory from the time individuals are the pursuers to the time they become the pursued. Given this scenario, *ganas*, the desire to ensure a level playing field by doing the right things, does not end at the entrance door. With a keen understanding that attracting diverse talent is only the starting point for a fully inclusive, participatory workforce, motivated managers know that talent development and advancement potential *are* at the heart of the matter. That's what will keep the workplace entrants from exiting prematurely.

Faced with internal and external pressures to diversify more quickly, some heartfelt employers turn to outside hiring for an immediate infusion of diverse perspectives in the mid- and senior-management ranks. However, they fully understand that this is just a short-term fix; for to have lasting results they must ensure that the pipelines to the top don't leak diverse talent for reasons such as attitudinal bias or prejudice. Regardless of the level at the point of entry, all aspects of the employment process — compensation, initial placement, job title, reporting relationships, scope of duties and responsibilities — must be carefully reviewed to ensure they are free from gender, race, or any other consideration that is based on prohibitive personal characteristics.

Surveys continue to affirm that individuals who perceived unfairness of any kind, even if due to a basis not covered by existing laws, such as nepotism or favoritism, are less satisfied with their jobs and their companies. Regrettably, all forms of bias and prejudice continue to exist in the workplace today. Inspired managers recognize these tendencies, but work to eradicate them on a daily basis. With guidance and direction from HR professionals, line managers must monitor actions and decisions to ensure that there are no institutional, cultural, or policy impediments to the open, inclusive, and unfiltered flow of talent. Focused on success, heartfelt leaders will develop "check points" to ensure fairness, especially in terms of talent development and advancement (see Figure 5.1). Instituting accountability measures at all entry points within the organization will enhance workplace fairness.

Growing diverse talent from within an organization is the truest measure of a well designed, fairly administered set of policies and procedures accessible to all. The efforts associated with developing diverse talent and identifying credential-building opportunities must be comprehensive and all-inclusive. They must cut across the various HR functions and business operations. It is in the coordination of these efforts and the harmonious execution of these interactions that heartfelt leaders can make a positive difference and leave a lasting legacy of fairness and inclusion.

Figure 5.1

Talent Development Check Points

- Formal Onboarding Experiences
- Unbiased Performance Assessments
- Face Time with Senior Management
- Special Projects and Task Force Assignments
- Leadership Role(s)
- Rotational Assignments and Exposures
- Promotional Opportunities
- External Development Opportunities

Onboarding as a Form of Training

Over the years we have had the opportunity to work with many companies, both looking in as federal officials and looking within as consultants. One company that we audited invested significantly in its college recruitment program, only to find out that three years later, over 50 percent of its recruits had left to pursue other opportunities. When a few of the professionals of color who had stayed with the company were interviewed, we learned that there was a sense of uncertainty, of loneliness, of not being sure they belonged, because, as one put it "no one has reached out to us to let us know that they care about our future here."

After successfully recruiting a diverse pool of new recruits, HR professionals and the line manager must now work together to ensure their successful entry, or "onboarding." Onboarding refers to the process of integrating new employees to the workplace and providing them with the tools and exposures necessary to succeed. Strategic processes might include:

» Formal or informal mentoring;
» Meetings with senior management;
» Career shadowing;
» Organizational training;
» Rotational assignments; and
» Utilization of networking/affinity groups.

Such interactions promote professional growth, build trust and alliances, and provide a seamless transition to that all-important "hand off" of customers and responsibilities when the time comes for senior members of the team to move on. Job sharing, job overlap, or any other practice that allows for the sharing of responsibilities makes for a smoother and more comfortable passage, providing customers with the assurance that they continue to be in good hands.

Successful onboarding can result in a 31 percent increase in employee retention, 24 percent increase in time to productivity for new hires, and a 31 percent increase in employee engagement.[3] Top performing companies have over 75 percent of their new employees participate in onboarding experiences, resulting in higher productivity, higher customer satisfaction and cost savings.[4] Human Resources would be well served to apply onboarding techniques beyond new hires to include those recently promoted or transferred, as well as those "on loan" through temporary assignments, in order to also foster successful transitions in these cases. Such onboarding techniques in these promotional/transfer situations could include:

» Formal orientation sessions;

» The use of an informal "buddy" system (assigning a co-worker to help with entry into the new area or unit);

» Formal mentoring; and,

» Team assignments.

Career Advancement Opportunities: Posting and Job Boards

In most workplace settings, vacancy notices are posted on internal job boards or electronic posting systems. A few companies claim to post openings all the way up to the CEO's direct reports level. Most companies, however, post up to the mid- to upper-middle management ranks. By coupling the posting of vacancies with well-defined position requirements, employers have realized greater transparency to the staffing process and created a sense of open competition toward advancement. Companies undergoing restructures and realignments have also used this approach and found it to have alleviated employee relations issues. By requiring incumbents to reapply and compete for their current position, or for any other position they deemed appropriate, and by putting them through the same rigorous interview and application process as any other applicant, management has been able to upgrade requisite skills through the non-selection of those no longer meeting the updated criteria. HR professionals then have the opportunity to provide remedial training and retool talent in those instances where skills gaps become evident.

Posting systems, when managed honestly and with integrity, foster feelings of fairness and promote a level playing field. Without such, employers not only lose credibility, but also could face liability. Examples abound. Clara Watson, a black teller at a bank in Texas, claimed that she applied for promotional opportunities but was repeatedly passed over in favor of whites. The bank failed to show that

Watson was less qualified than those who were promoted, as there were no objective criteria. Additionally, the bank failed to show that its promotional processes were objective and based upon validated selection procedures.[5] Regular review of duties and responsibilities and evaluation of requirements, along with the visible advancement of diverse talent will build trust in the system and allay concerns of subjective favoritism. On position announcements, *ganas*-focused leaders will:

» Clearly describe duties and responsibilities;

» Specify qualifications required;

» Validate tests if administered; and

» Encourage all interested and eligible to apply.

"The Tap, the Nod, or the Wiring"

Even where the posting of vacancies is a corporate policy, it is not unusual for managers to transfer or promote individuals outside the formal process. While such actions might not be discriminatory on the surface — and most employers understand the need to fill vacancies in a timely manner and allow such practices on an "exception to the rule" basis — when "the tap" or "the nod" consistently goes to a homogeneous group of team members, the practice could undermine the heartfelt leader's efforts to promote diversity. Employees know these practices take place. While management might think, "No one will notice if I give Steve the comptroller position," rest assured, Stephanie, Carlos, and Mariah — all equally qualified — will notice. Similarly, some job postings include the reference, "candidate identified." Such a reference will have a chilling effect on the application process, as prospective candidates will inevitably believe that the position is already "wired." HR professionals should work closely with line managers to minimize these instances. At a minimum, they should monitor and review the list of candidates identified to ensure that, once again, they are not being drawn from a homogeneous pool.

Cartoon 5.1

"Why is it when a job posting says 'she' it's never for management positions?"

The Benchmarking of Talent

Employers are always interested in knowing how their internal talent measures up to the talent available in the marketplace. It is common for an employer to post a job internally while also conducting an external search. In these instances, it is recommended that documentation be very specific as to the disposition of all internal candidates and external applicants to ensure a fair comparison and an inclusive process. Growing leaders from within makes economic sense, fosters continuity, and ensures a better cultural fit than going externally. Such growth should be managed by defining core competencies, identifying high-potential talent, providing honest assessments of the talent base, creating individualized development plans, and tracking progress and milestones.[6] Even those employers who pride themselves on having a strong "promote from within" culture find themselves facing onboarding issues and talent tension when they hire uniquely qualified individuals from the outside, or when they merge with, or acquire, another company. Heartfelt leaders value loyalty and dedication and resist the tendency to depreciate the familiar, in-house talent, even though market pressures can sometimes influence a different choice.

Career Planning and Development

Career planning today is a strategic business objective. There are as many variations of the process as there are companies. And there are equally as many ways for capturing and managing the development of talent, including the drafting of individual development plans (IDPs), high-potential lists, key contributor lists, value box assessments, and succession plans, as well as the tracking of performance results, rankings, and growth potential evaluations. For many, the C-suite drives the process, planning and guiding the developmental assignments and advancement of those in upper middle management. For others, executive management could dip a bit further down into the management ranks. Even in those companies where almost all job vacancies are posted, the process is carefully managed. Like a chess game, the "pieces" are handpicked, moved around, and strategically placed to ensure success. In some cases, the selected individual might have come out of a carefully drafted, frequently updated succession plan. In other cases, the individuals selected might have never appeared on any formal plan or written list. Instead, they captured the attention of a senior manager who directed the assignment or strongly encouraged the acceptance of the opportunity being offered. In spite of the extraordinary efforts devoted to developing succession plans and creating lists, their usage has been inconsistent.

One of the challenges that the maintenance of these programs poses is keeping up with the fast pace of change. Leadership changes and a shifting business environment can make these plans obsolete overnight. At a company where the previous CEO retired, the new CEO brought with him an entirely new team of managers and a different set of expectations for advancement, making the sophisticated systems that had been in place earlier totally irrelevant. This is common in today's dramatic business transformations.

Developed, but Not Advanced

Another challenge that employees face is overcoming past slip-ups — e.g., a project that went awry, a presentation that did not go well, or a difference of opinions with an individual now in a high-level position of influence — which can affect their chances for advancement. "These people don't forget and don't recognize that we change and learn from our experiences," said one mid-level executive at a major company. Some corporate cultures have long memories. Through word of mouth, incidents of long ago are kept alive, derailing opportunities for those involved. Employees complain of their inability to shed their "corporate baggage" and of the lack of opportunity for a fresh start. Women and professionals of color, relatively new to organizational politics, are particularly vulnerable to derailments without the support of a coach or mentor. Inspired leaders, working in concert with HR professionals, can help overcome these earlier missteps by asking:

» "How can we get 'Jordan' engaged again?"
» "What did Jordan learn from the experience that could help him in the future?"
» "Would a mentor or coach help Jordan navigate?"
» "Can we find a champion for Jordan in upper-level management?"

Diversity and Talent Development

While the diversity officer and the office of talent development might be separate HR tracks in many settings, a number of companies have combined the functions of diversity and talent development under one officer. This is in recognition of the competitive advantage businesses gain by growing diverse talent in a global economy. It could also be a reflection of past failures, when diversity and talent development ran on parallel tracks, only to meet by accident. Talent development policies institute what the C-suite values. The organizational culture is represented in those that it is grooming. The *ganas*-led leader:

» Ensures that all developmental lists are inclusive of qualified diverse talent;

» Drives accountability for the composition of succession plans and talent pools; and,

» Actively taps diverse talent for career-building assignments.

HR professionals can protect the integrity of the employer's commitment to inclusion and diversity by ensuring the full and complete review and discussion of *every* individual eligible for developmental consideration.

A Case in Point

"I call it the 'Mini-Me' syndrome. Executives seem to feel more comfortable when critical organizational roles are filled by people who are similar to the incumbent. That resemblance is often manifested in age, education, leadership style, industry experience, career trajectory, and, of course, race and gender." — Diversity consultant

Developmental Opportunities

"My success was a direct result of an assignment to turn around an office that was in a condemned building and had a 45% vacancy rate in the management team. I re-staffed, reorganized and relocated the office to great success."
— Retired female state director

The *ganas*-driven executive fully appreciates that while progress has been made in the quest for an open and inclusive workplace, much still remains to be done. Studies attest to that fact. Recently, researchers from the Kellogg Graduate School of Management and Loyola University's Institute of Human Resources & Industrial Relations found that women's salaries and frequency of job transfers lagged behind their male peers at 20 *Fortune* 500 companies even though they had similar education, employment without breaks, were open to transfer, worked in similar industries and had similar levels of family power and support, undercutting the human capital and family power theories of wage differentials.[7] Such studies only validate what many women and people of color feel every day on a personal level — in their workplaces.

In those organizations where transfers and lateral reassignments are used for developmental purposes, the HR professional must ensure that everyone, including women and people of color, understands the expectations. At times, Human Resources must go the extra mile to counsel and advise them as to the merits of such an opportunity. It could be that stereotypes are preventing the woman or professional of color from accepting the assignment. An obvious example is the use of executive assistant (EA) positions. In some settings, the EA is a future leader or successor apparent. In this role, the EA hones interpersonal skills while gaining face time with executives and becoming educated on a broader range of issues. In other workplaces, the EA is administrative, prioritizing paperwork and serving as a "gatekeeper" to the executive. Understanding how one's organization uses these openings is important to deciding whether to accept them. At a minimum, the exposure to a broader circle of contacts and activities will better equip the high-potential candidate, but determining whether the benefits will far outweigh the other considerations involving such a move must be examined on a case-by-case basis.

Inspired leaders do not send employees out on cross-functional, developmental assignments on a wish and a prayer. Rather, they understand the need for structure and set deliverables as a desirable outcome of the opportunity. "People are often sent on assignment with the hope that, while accomplishing the task set before them, they will learn wisdom, insight, and improved judgment."[8] Working with Human Resources, *ganas*-motivated leaders will guide, encourage, and provide the feedback required for professional growth.

Effective development plans are customized to the individual needs. A line executive might need a greater working knowledge of the roles that human resources and community relations play in the overall corporate strategy. Or, a mid-level manager might need profit & loss (P&L) responsibilities. Historically, women and people of color who have advanced to executive positions have done so through staff rather than line roles.[9] Yet, the path to the company's highest level, the chief executive office suite, is through line responsibilities in most cases. Over the years, some progress has been made in getting women and professionals of color into substantive line positions. Nevertheless, these groups continue to be largely concentrated in staff positions, and not always by choice.

"I was in a line job overseas. I moved the troops, the equipment. I had a lot of responsibility and was due for a promotion. I was told I was being promoted to a position back stateside. When I arrived at my new base I was a glorified clerical. When I went to another black officer to ask what I should do he cautioned me not to rock the boat … that I had the promotion and should let it go or else I'd damage my career." — Black female military officer

Understanding that these line experiences are critical to advancement, motivated leaders actively promote the inclusion of women, people with disabilities, and ethnically and racially diverse groups for such opportunities.

Education and Learning

Each year employers spend millions of dollars on education and learning. These learning opportunities take many forms — from online courses designed to enhance knowledge and skills from the comfort of one's computer, to in-house classroom sessions intended to strengthen functional and management expertise, to the more formal external education programs offered by major universities and leading institutes on thought leadership and other state-of-the-art issues. Together, these programs and courses not only stimulate development but also provide perspective and motivation. Ensuring the open and fair apportionment of these learning opportunities, and removing barriers affecting participation can further diversity and inclusion at all levels of employment. HR professionals are uniquely suited for this task.

Some companies encourage but do not require employees to take online courses. However, when promotional opportunities arise, selecting officials might look at the individual's employment history to evaluate motivation and self-direction. An absence of participation in these courses could affect selection when compared to other candidates who have enlisted. HR professionals can provide informal coaching and counseling to enlighten employees as to the value of these courses beyond their technical implications. Similarly, heartfelt managers should seize every opportunity to encourage lifelong learning and advocate participation. Those with limited exposure to organizational subtleties often miss the importance of these programs — the recognition that everything a company provides has a purpose and a connection to other actions and decisions that it takes.

At the supervisory and managerial levels, participation in these programs is more structured and mandatory. Teaching managers how to interview and provide performance feedback, for example, not only develops skills but also avoids liability. Companies offer core course requirements for this segment of the workforce, and monitor participation closely to ensure that *everyone* in these positions, regardless of race or gender, understand their roles and the potential consequences of their actions.

At the highest levels of corporate learning, the process, once again, becomes more subjective and voluntary, but the stakes are higher. Not signing up means not being eligible for advancement to the next level. Upper middle managers might be encouraged but not required to attend executive development courses that could take them away from time-sensitive projects and families for two to three weeks at a time. It is common to find less participation of women in these programs, even though they know the consequences. The hardship associated with being away from home and family hits women disproportionately more. Some have small children, others are single parents, and still others are sandwiched between caring for children and elderly parents. So they put it off.

"I'm single and don't have a family, but my mother has dementia. She relies on me for everything. I could get away for a week or so, but it is very difficult to be gone longer than that." — Female upper management executive

The policy that "all must attend these courses for advancement, but it is up to you," while neutral on its face, more adversely affects certain groups of managers, namely women and women of color. HR professionals can relieve some of the pressures facing women by:

> » Revisiting the purpose and objectives of these programs;
> » Reporting the impact of participation requirements on the various groups;
> » Encouraging executive managers to be flexible and adaptable to mitigating circumstances; and,
> » Redesigning the programs to allow for a more modular education model that meets the stated objectives but does so without imposing long absences from home.

Heartfelt leaders not only concern themselves with the exigencies of the business but also with the personal balance that individuals must strike to be productive while still pursuing their professional aspirations. Managers motivated by the twin goals of inclusion and diversity understand that it takes their active, direct intervention to set the course for the development of future leaders and ensure that valuable contributors are not missing out of opportunities because of policies and practices that can be remedied.

Testing and Assessment Centers

When queried as to how women and people of color fare in personality tests and leadership potential, one executive clarified that they might have "more opportunities for improvement, but no one fails."

The competitive nature of our economy has made top talent a rare commodity. Beyond executive education and other forms of learning, more and more employers are using testing and assessment centers as a way to evaluate talent and determine its suitability for higher-level positions. Employers, protective of their organizational culture, will have proprietary assessment tests designed to measure the compatibility of a candidate or a high-potential individual with the company's values and preferred personal qualities. There are simulated exercises conducted to gauge how individuals will operate under intense pressure, or how they will respond when faced with conflicting interests of ethics and profits. A command of organizational values is essential to passing these tests with high marks. Some do well with the analytical, intelligence quotients, but fail on the emotional, temperamental components of the tests, when matched against company standards. Others experience the opposite, falling short of expectations in the mastery of "hard knowledge and skills." Given the makeup of the workforce at these levels, the majority of the population tested is typically male and white, with a sprinkling of women and people of color making the cut.

The use of tests and test validation processes at these highly subjective levels have been getting a lot of attention and notice by the federal government. Many predict that this will be the next big wave of federal scrutiny in the pursuit of nondiscrimination. As this practice becomes more commonplace, HR professionals must be alert to its potential pitfalls. Women and people of color undergoing these assessments could be at a disadvantage if they haven't fully grasped the essence of what the company values, either because of limited networking, access, exposure, or lack of mentoring to fill in the gaps of cultural knowledge. An appropriate course of action for HR professionals working in confidence with senior executives might be to:

» Increase their visibility and networking opportunities;
» Promote more informal mentoring;

» Ensure the validation of tests for adverse impact on the basis of race, gender, or ethnicity;

» Evaluate the subsequent performance of those executives who "passed" with high marks and moved on to more responsible positions — how did they do compared to those who didn't test as well?

» Provide recommendations for leveling the playing field to ensure full access and inclusion of diverse talent.

The Mobility Factor

"I took this job because I was told there was adequate medical care for my son who has autism. It wasn't until I got here that I learned that meant a 3-hour drive to the city. That might not sound bad, and wouldn't be if you were healthy and talking about an annual physical, but the frequent drive on poor roads to see his therapist and specialists is a killer for my wife." — Executive expatriate

One of the most frequently asked questions during interviews is, "Are you mobile?" Being mobile has come to represent flexibility and willingness to do whatever it takes to get the job done on behalf of one's company. In the old days, "IBMers" used to joke that the company's acronym stood for "I've Been Moved (again)." In the IBM culture and that of its many peer companies, being mobile meant moving up. Individuals might be able to turn down a relocation request without lasting consequences, but by turning down the second or third request, they would run the risk of not being asked again, of "falling off the fast track" and being replaced by someone else more mobile. Often the transfers in and out of corporate headquarters allowed the C-suite to measure the employee's professional development and commitment to the company.

Today, with 68 percent of multinational companies surveyed stating that they expect to ramp up their overseas employee assignments,[10] mobility has once again become an important factor in career advancement. But the complexities involved in taking on these assignments have also grown. An increase of double-income couples, along with family considerations and concerns about re-entry and next steps have made these decisions very difficult to make.

Three Human Resources areas of concern surrounding globalization are (1) finding suitable expatriate candidates; (2) helping them and their families complete the assignment; and (3) retaining them once their assignment ends. Inspired leaders will work to ensure that such opportunities are open to all qualified talent, without presumptions based on gender, marital status, or any other personal characteristics. That is to say, opportunities will not only be offered to qualified talent on an unbiased basis, but sincere efforts will be made to encourage acceptance and ensure success in the assignment.

Human Resources plays key roles in all three areas by:

» Identifying diverse candidates with the skills set and motivation to both support the company's efforts and personally draw benefit from the experience;

» Working with the families to also prepare them for the assignment — familiarizing them with customs, language, schooling options, cooking, safety, and other valuable tips for a successful transition; and

» Facilitating a smooth re-entry upon completion of the assignment.

Following the completion of an assignment, expectations run high, and re-entry into one's home base can turn into a bit of a culture shock: The organization might not look or feel the same, and management changes and the passage of time might have taken a toll on previously established professional networks and relationships. Worse, the position available might not be the one anticipated. The risk of losing this valuable talent to outside interests could become quite real if the re-entry is not properly managed. HR professionals and heartfelt leaders empathize and, working together, provide a "landing cushion" through special assignments and other high-profile roles, until the appropriate opportunity becomes available.

Successful Succession

Diversity has been credited with creating new business opportunities, strengthening our leadership and competitive standing in the global marketplace, and enhancing the overall quality of customer service. Some years ago, IBM sent to Spain the first woman ever to preside over its operations in that country. In a culture where business dealings were considered the realm of men, and women were predominantly found in support roles, this action created quite a stir. The story goes that upon meeting the woman executive, an agitated Spanish official called IBM's corporate offices and clamored: "You sent us a *woman*!" To which the senior executive responded, "No, we sent you the *best*." That act of courage, that *ganas*-led action, opened the doors of opportunity for many similar firsts around the world, and forever expanded the base of talent to include the very best of both genders, for the economic benefit of all.

A recent four-year study of return on equity (ROE) and total return to shareholders (TRS) of more than 300 *Fortune* 500 companies identified that the companies with the highest representation of women in senior management had 35 percent higher ROE and 34 percent higher TRS when compared against companies having the lowest representation of women. The study reportedly controlled for industry and corporate differences. "Business leaders increasingly request hard data to support the link between gender diversity and corporate performance. This study gives business leaders unquestionable evidence that a link does exist."[12]

Motivated managers do not need studies or spreadsheets to listen to their inner voices. They instinctively understand that to exclude human talent from advancement for reasons as irrelevant or immaterial as race, gender, ethnicity, or any other personal characteristic, is not only economically inefficient and wasteful but also immoral and at odds with the values that make our nation so great. The successful succession process cannot survive without these guiding beliefs. As difficult as it is to choose from the "best of the best" talent available in an inclusive, balanced manner, nothing tests the mettle of an inspired leader more than assessing employee performance that cuts across all other HR decisions.

06 Heart to Heart

"Commitment to diversity and inclusion are critical to becoming an employer of choice and winning the war for talent, as well as being a preferred business partner and place to shop."
— Jeanine Jones[1]

Heartfelt Leader

A *Fortune* 200 company, known for routinely monitoring every employment policy and practice, was caught off-guard during a discussion on how best to handle an economic downturn. During the C-suite discussion of a reduction in force, using performance as the determining factor for downsizing was put on the table. What seemed like the easiest, cleanest way of reducing staff became one executive's nightmare when a reduction of those rated at the bottom of the rating scale (a 4) was offered. While the company self-audited routinely to ensure management stayed within the rating guidelines, it did not check to ensure that those rated 1 were in fact exemplary; those rated 3 average or new to grade; and those rated 4 were needing improvement. The executive team had an "aha moment" when it learned that this executive routinely filled the 4 rating category with his high fliers moving quickly through the system, promoting them without question and allowing him more room in the other 3 categories. If this policy had been accepted, this executive would have lost his best and brightest. *It is best to routinely "check under the hood,"* *as even the best of systems can be called into question.*

Review. Rate. Reward. Retain.

Heartfelt leaders understand that measuring, assessing, and conveying performance in a meaningful, constructive manner are some of management's most important obligations. Of all the HR practices in use, performance management is one of the most time-consuming, as countless hours are devoted to designing and implementing, communicating, retooling, and guiding the process. Performance management must be inherently culture-based to be effective, as behaviors are rewarded that further the organization's goals and vision while also positively affecting bottom-line results. Regardless of whether assessments are: performed on an annual basis by anniversary date or a common date; conducted quarterly or semi-annually; narrative-based; narrative-based coupled with ratings, rankings, or other quantifiers; or, approved and concurred upon by higher-level management, the issues are the same: Measure. Assess. Convey.

While some advocate a very simple performance assessment, others have moved to multiple ratings, multiple reviewers, and higher management concurrence (even if the higher up executives have no oversight of the individuals themselves). Forced ratings, which set maximum rating percentages allowed within each performance level; ratings that must conform to a bell-shaped curve; or forced rankings, which require the rater to compare employees and determine the relative ordering on performance, for example, constrict line management's discretion even further.

As is the case with all employment processes, there are some who are apprehensive about performance assessments, employees and management alike. Whether it is employee anxiety from being compared with peers, or the simple fact that this HR function takes time away from competing demands causing trepidation for the line manager, this HR function has many detractors. Others think differently: "Many employees actually look forward to their performance appraisal," as it provides them a chance to gain recognition and reward; receive appreciation; resolve grievances; identify objectives to help their career; and identify areas that require greater management support.[2]

For management, performance must be captured and relayed in a manner that is objective, fair, and consistent. Its importance cannot be overstated, as it forms the basis for base salary decisions, bonus decisions, other forms of compensation (stock and other long-term incentives), promotional opportunities, developmental opportunities, career advancement, and even retention. Ensuring that performance assessments are honest, consistent, unbiased, and objective is an ongoing challenge, for the process is carried out by multitudes of managers nationwide who, on any given day, might be biased, prejudiced by events or influenced by others.

Record Performance, Not Perceptions

Performance assessment is not a practice used by all employers, with 34 percent of employees surveyed stating they never or rarely have had them, and 20 percent of management reporting the same.[3] It can, however, further the goals of the organization while providing employees a framework by which they can reflect, take action, and improve.

Pay for performance is today's leading compensation philosophy as employers focus on the bottom-line, doing more with less, higher production, return on investment, and shareholder value. But, do employers really pay for performance? It depends upon whom you ask. Employers like the concept, but admit that there are impediments to full implementation, including lack of sufficient discretionary funds to make an impact. Employers that report successful pay for performance systems in place tend to come from younger, less-hierarchical organizations with several remuneration vehicles from which to choose to reward performance. Employees often believe that it is their length of service that primarily determines their pay, and that there is simply not enough money available to make a dramatic difference in compensation based upon merit or performance.

As more positions become thought-based rather than production-related, discretion in rating or ranking performance becomes more subjective. With industrial psychologists proffering theories such as the halo effect (that management is biased in a positive fashion toward an employee so much that it colors all else) or the horn effect (that management only can recall the negative aspects of an employee's performance regardless of other results), coupled with other forms of rater bias, how can an employer ensure internal equity and fairness?

One study a few years ago offered that the gap between the advancement of men and women in the workplace was due to traditional views held by mid- and senior-level men. A new study regarding societal roles carries this same tenet to the world of compensation. According to a longitudinal study by organizational psychologists, men with traditional views about the "woman's place in the world" were paid the most, far outpacing the others. While the study was based upon men and women working in the same jobs, with the same levels of education and working the same number of hours per week, men with egalitarian attitudes were found to earn more than women with egalitarian views, but the wage gap between the men with traditional attitudes and women with traditional attitudes was ten times that of the difference between men and women with egalitarian views.[4]

When the performance management system requires assessment on subjective items such as "leadership abilities" or "perceived potential" for employees who are not in senior roles, how can managers perform such reviews honestly? With the evolution of performance management from skills to perceived competencies such as problem solving, how can a manager compare individuals across job titles and units?

The *ganas* for honesty and integrity drives heartfelt managers to do so in as transparent a manner as the company allows. Even in those settings where ratings or rankings are kept confidential from the employee, heartfelt managers go the extra mile to provide honest feedback in a forthright manner on not only strengths and areas for improvement, but training, development, and supplementary exposures, which could strengthen weaknesses. In turn, such managers turn out to be the most valuable of mentors — not formal, assigned career guides, but informal, honest assessors of talent and needs.

No matter what the performance management system, employees quickly gauge "what matters most" and perform according to those measures. Performance objectives that are set in a clear, concise language and conveyed to the engaged employee in a constructive manner will enhance productivity and satisfaction.

The costs of any form of performance assessment system can be staggering. One manager of a company of 130,000 employees estimated the cost of preparing appraisals, setting goals and objectives, and conducting interim and annual performance reviews, at about $100 million per year — even though he assumed that only 60 percent of the employees would receive assessments.[5] Add to these costs other performance assessment expenses such as review time at higher levels, designing/printing/copying/ distributing appraisal forms, designing and communicating the appraisal process, training, and handling employee relations issues, and the costs become exorbitant.

A Case in Point

"I never know where I stand. I get good verbal feedback at my annual appraisal and never have heard of weaknesses, even when I ask. Yet, I'm never left in charge of the office, and haven't had a promotion in years. I know I need to broaden out and handle other accounts, but I never get the jobs when I apply. I'm thinking I need to leave the company in order to move up. It's too bad because I really like my friends here." — Female financial analyst

Results of Bias in Performance Management

The motivated manager will instill accountabilities to ensure that bias does not influence the process. From spot-checking narratives for gender-biased language or use of racial or cultural references, to reviewing the correlation between narratives and ratings and rankings, to ensuring that there is no statistical disparity in ratings affecting any particular group, motivated managers work to make certain there is truly an equal playing field throughout.

Independent research suggests that such reviews can uncover statistical disparities. Jacqueline Landau conducted a study that concluded that race (white) and gender (male) were both tied to significantly higher ratings in a sampling of 1,268 managers and employees. After controlling for age, tenure, education, salary grade, functional area, and satisfaction with career support, Landau found that women were rated lower than men, and blacks and Asians were rated lower than whites.[6]

If a review of performance results identifies a statistical disparity adversely affecting a particular group of employees, further research is warranted to isolate the policy, the practice, or the rater(s) causing such disparity. Having a disparity is not in and of itself discriminatory. It is, however, a red flag that requires further investigation to make sure it is not caused by attitudinal biases emanating from the corporate culture or from individual managers. No matter how often Human Resources explains what to assess and how to assess it, whenever the human element is introduced, there is an opportunity for error. *Ganas* pulls at the motivated manager to ensure fairness. Regardless of the type of performance management system in place, the fact that such forms the basis for so many decisions down the line beckons to inspired managers. Honesty must be integral to the assessment and feedback; fairness must guide all ratings and rankings; and the written documentation must have integrity in and of itself such that all future decisions predicated upon it will withstand further scrutiny.

The Pay Is the Thing!

A strong emotional association exists between pay and an employee's sense of self-worth. Because the marketplace sets the price for one's skills, abilities, and experiences, pay reflects what an employee is deemed to be worth to the company in a supply and demand economy. For employees, compensation is personal. It is not just about their pay; it is about their worth to the employers, and therefore triggers an emotional reaction. Surveys consistently rank money as less important to employee satisfaction than working for caring managers or having a good working environment. Yet pay that is commensurate to one's role and responsibilities in an organization can serve as a strong motivator of performance. Pay is also a source of poor relations and disputes in the workplace. Part of the concern with pay could be inadequate communication between the employer and the employee. "If employees understand their rewards, they will value them and be more engaged in the business, which will realize more value for the dollars invested in the total rewards programs. The company will also likely see lower turnover and improved financial performance."[7]

Just as there are some employers who don't assess performance in a formal, written manner, so too are there employers who do not have a compensation system for establishing base pay, providing bonuses or other incentives, or determining perquisites. Most readers might assume these employers to be very small businesses, yet they often employ more than 50 employees, a sizable number. When there is no "system" in place, allegations of biased compensation are harder to defend. When there is no compensation system and no performance assessment system and bias or discrimination is alleged, the employer who simply "knows his/her employees and how they perform," and grants pay increases and bonuses accordingly, will have a difficult time in a courtroom.

With women earning $0.77 to the dollar that men make in the United States,[8] managers motivated by the drive for internal equity work to ensure that there are lawful reasons for differentiation within the workplace. While some claim that pay differentials are not based on bias, but rather on chosen career paths, education, time off, and other quantifiable factors, undertaking pay equity studies to really identify the causes is often discouraged for fear of exposure and liability.

> "Many, perhaps most, employers today believe they behave fairly toward women and men. They believe and say that they hire, pay and promote each individual worker according to her or his education, experience, capacities, and merits. And yet I've heard of very few employers racing forward to prove that no wage gap exists under their corporate rooftop or to audit the books to see if such a gap is there — or, if they notice that a wage gap does exist, examining and fixing personnel practices to get rid of it. Many employers do know that the men are getting paid more than the women. But not a single boss would blame himself (or, for that matter, herself)."[9]

Ensuring that compensation decisions are fair and equitable continues to be the law of the land. However, as compensation practices have been among the most guarded of corporate information, with employees routinely signing nondisclosure and non-compete clauses at time of hire or during onboarding, there has been limited access or transparency to these processes. Executive management, with only the most trusted of advisors having full and unfettered access to the data, carefully guards compensation actions. Heartfelt leaders are sensitive to the possibilities of pay inequities and work to ensure transparency and to eliminate non-job-related salary differences.

Nondiscrimination in compensation was the focus of the first bill signed into law by President Barack Obama. By signing the Fair Pay Act, President Obama sent a powerful message that his administration would not tolerate vestiges of past discriminatory practices, no matter when those practices took place. The Fair Pay Act was a direct legislative response to the Supreme Court decision in *Ledbetter v. Goodyear Tire & Rubber Co., Inc.*[10] In the case, Lilly Ledbetter alleged that she was discriminated against in compensation at Goodyear Tire & Rubber because of her gender while employed, but that she didn't realize that discrimination had taken place until after her retirement from the company. The Supreme Court found in favor of Goodyear. It stated that the discriminatory behavior *Ledbetter* had alleged occurred long before her retirement, exceeding the statutory time limits for filing a complaint. However, in passing the Fair Pay Act, Congress extended the period by which compensation discrimination claims can be made against employers such that each new paycheck (or annuity payment) re-starts the 180-day time clock to file for discrimination. It also holds employers liable for management decisions for which there might be no records.

Are There More Ledbetters Out There?

Though the Supreme Court did not expressly rule on the merits of Lilly Ledbetter's compensation case, but only on the timely filing issues, if employers do not routinely review compensation decisions there could indeed be more Ledbetters in the making. If remuneration decisions are kept private for institutional reasons of confidentiality and trade secrets, employers wishing to truly inspire inclusion and good corporate stewardship should monitor their compensation decisions on an annual basis such that a *Ledbetter* situation does not occur. Employers working with Human Resources and the general counsel's office should examine past practices and the continuing effect of such past practices to eliminate potential disparities that could have been caused by gender, race, or any other prohibitive factor. The deadline for filing a claim starts anew each time an employee receives wages, benefits, or other compensation that could reflect vestiges of past discriminatory pay practices. Back pay and other remedies could be assessed dating back to two years from the date a charge was filed with the EEOC. The political publicity that the *Ledbetter* decision created and the subsequent passage of the Fair Pay Act have heightened awareness to this issue, thus increasing the likelihood that more charges of this nature will be filed. Employers would be prudent to review their previous pay practices. Employees are counting on such vigilance.

Simple Analyses

There are innumerable consultants, statisticians, and compensation gurus who work with clients on multiple regression analyses to determine if there are large, statistical imbalances in all forms of compensation. And while such analyses might be impressive, they are not without detractors who argue as to the type of modeling, the number of standard deviations, the confidence level used, the variables utilized, and whether the variables are tainted. Additionally, many employers find that the information they need to explain or defend their compensation data is not readily available (or kept current) in the human resource information system (HRIS). Thus, when an internal audit is requested, or the federal government comes calling, there is a flurry of activity to identify which variables might "explain away" salary differentials — even if these same variables are not utilized in determining salaries.

There are some basic analyses that can be used no matter how simple or complicated the compensation system. "Outliers" — individuals whose compensation is far above or below the rest — tend to skew analyses no matter the format or complexity. It has been our experience that in most cases it is the outliers who skew the compensation analyses no matter how you cut the data. Below are some of these data analyses.

Starting Salaries

Differentials in starting salaries are almost impossible to rectify in organizations in which salary increases and cost-of-living increases are minimal. All things being equal, having one's salary placed lower in the salary range often necessitates lower bonuses, as bonuses are often a percentage of base salary tied to one's performance rating or ranking. Some of the questions worthy of review include:

» Is there a differential in starting salaries between groups or classes of new hires? That is to say, if you've onboarded 20 new hires from MBA programs nationwide, is there much variation in starting salaries? If so, does it favor or disadvantage a particular gender or racial group? If so, a review of salary determinations is in order.

» Is there a differential between the starting salaries of the few high-level managers onboarded compared to others in the same pay grade, title or organizational level? Recall the issues raised in Chapter 4 when new hires at the higher levels of management cause salary inequities with others. Is this justified? What was the executive's salary that vacated? Is it similar to the new hire? It should be noted that when a new hire is compensated much higher than those in the same position and pay band, other issues arise.

Below the Minimum

When a pay system has any type of maximum or minimum per title, grade, job family, or band, one should review all those whose salaries are below the minimum of the band to which they are assigned. Even if these are "the exception to the rule" or a "new hire" or "new to grade," it is important to review these compared to others in the pay grade.

» Regardless of the reason, what is the demographic composition of those who fall below the minimum of the range?

» Why were these new hires placed below the minimum? Were others placed directly into the pay band? What is the demographic composition of the new hires whose salaries fall below the minimum and the new hires whose salaries fall within the band?

» If the compensation strategy is to give a standard percentage increase to all of those who were "new to grade" does the policy cause a disadvantage to one group or another below the minimum of the range?

Above the Maximum

Much like the other analyses, those above the maximum of the salary range will skew any review of base pay. While some might be found here due to red circling of base pay when demoting or reorganizing positions, others are here due to time in pay range and out of the ordinary pay increases.

» Regardless of the reason, what is the demographic composition of all those found above the maximum? Are they being compensated according to guidelines? Are "exceptions to the rule" continuing?

» How large were the salary increases given to employees at these levels? Were there any individuals whose increase was more than that allowed by policy (i.e., receiving an increase when the policy is to not provide such if above the maximum)?

Bright Line

While the above are some rough cuts, there are other basic analyses that any employer can perform to see how individuals are faring. There is no one "bright line" or safe harbor test, but a simple review of all those found two standard deviations from the median or mean of the title, salary level, range, or pay grade will produce statistical outliers warranting review. These will most likely include the same individuals identified in the "above the maximum" or "below the minimum" analyses discussed above.

Managers with *ganas* for a fair, inclusive and diverse workforce might continue with other analyses to ensure all systems are working equitably for all. Such analyses could include average merit increases by pay grade or level, current ratings tied to merit increases, ratings tied to bonus amounts, or other sophisticated forms of pay evaluation.

Why Do Analyses?

"Nothing raises hackles as fiercely as a change in performance feedback methods, especially when they affect compensation decisions."[11]

There are some who prefer not to do compensation analyses. There always have been. With no *ganas* for internal equity or inclusion, these employers would prefer to expressly not know if pay issues exist. Whether influenced by a general counsel who has done a risk-risk analysis in which the risk of self-identifying a compensation issue that could be costly to rectify outweighs the risk of a government audit, or of an employee filing a grievance or complaint, these employers choose to take no action.

One extreme example is from "Larry." Writing in an online blog against the *Ledbetter* decision, Larry writes:

"February 16, 2009 at 4:18 pm. I have a better solution — don't hire women in areas which may get scrutinized — such as areas which have multiple positions of the same type. As long as the gov't. keeps its hands in my business, I'm going to do my best to keep it out. There are ways to bring up issues — through the company or otherwise — but keep the gov't. and more regulation out."

However, it is important to note that whether one chooses to be the inspired, proactive employer or one wishes to passively wait it out, compensation disparities present serious risk liabilities. The employer who identifies such and works toward remedying it in a timely manner is more likely to win the day and hearts of employees than the employer who simply chooses to ignore these concerns. Without such a review, managers could find themselves in the same situation as one of the country's largest jewelers, who in 2008 was found to have discriminated against thousands of employees in terms of pay and promotional opportunities.

The EEOC found that, "[the company] does this by maintaining a system for making promotion and compensation decisions that is excessively subjective, and through which [the company] has permitted or encouraged managers to deny female employees" equal pay and promotional opportunities.[13]

There are some employers today without a formal pay structure in place. No grades. No bands. No ranges. While one might believe this gives a bye on self-analysis and review, the fact that managers have a wide discretion in compensation decisions could yield even greater concerns. Consideration should be given to establishing written policies and guidance to ensure that managers' decisions are fair, equitable, and nondiscriminatory.

The *Ganas* to Do the Right Thing

Well before the Fair Pay Act, employers monitored compensation practices for internal equity — some as a result of a legal action, others due to the *ganas* for fairness in the workplace. Regardless of location, size, or industry, ensuring nondiscrimination is every employer's responsibility. Such analyses should include base pay, merit increases, bonuses, stock options, stock grants, other long-term incentives, and perquisites.

There are many motivated employers. One large consumer goods company routinely monitors ratings to ensure nondiscrimination, coupled with merit increases and bonuses for adherence to guidelines. A bank reviews all ratings and increases before they are conveyed, requesting performance assessments for those ratings called into question. An HR director in the state of California explains:

"We have two annual audits by independent firms, quarterly audits by our contracted CPA, and monthly HR audits of each department payroll. As a non-profit, we have chosen not to include merit increases in our pay structure and can only provide pay increases when our state and federal economies are stable, since every increase must be sustainable. We pay at or above minimum wage and are keen on compliance across the board. Granted, we (HR) may miss an OT half hour on rare occasions, but the employee is quickly notified and pay is rectified. My Executive Director is "hands on" and helps HR ensure we don't make the mistakes that the *Ledbetter* decision would pin point."[14]

The Heartache of Turnover

Employee retention is one of the most difficult challenges that a company faces. While quality employees leave voluntarily for a variety of reasons each year, the heartfelt employer understands that training, development, and cross-fertilization can help stem the tide. Diversity can also be a retention tool. In a survey with a scale measuring commitment to diversity and inclusion, 84 percent of those with a high diversity score plan to stay with the company, compared to those with a low diversity score.[15] Mirroring these results is the fact that those respondents who gave their company high diversity policy scores were much more likely to recommend their company.[16]

When the employer reaches the unfortunate decision that, for business reasons, a reduction in force or furlough must be put into effect, the heartfelt employer works to ensure that such steps are taken in a nondiscriminatory fashion. Working closely with HR professionals and legal counsel, line managers must review every decision to select out individuals to ensure fairness and nondiscrimination. Whatever methodology the employer uses, it must be carried out on a non-discriminatory manner and for sound business reasons. For example, if the employer is utilizing a last-in, first-out method of downsizing, but some managers "cherry pick" to retain a few new hires here and there, the methodology is called into question. Inconsistency and bias can yield unlawful discrimination.

Heartfelt leaders understand that any perception of bias in a reduction in force or restructuring effort will compromise the integrity and question the sincerity of all other employment decisions. HR professionals must be involved in these actions from the beginning, evaluating rationale, analyzing data, identifying problem areas, and advising line managers as to the possible consequences of actions that are unevenly applied and subjectively executed.

07 A Heart Check-up: Have You Hugged Your Policies Lately?

"You want our compensation manual? To find out how we actually pay people we'd better have a talk. What the manual says isn't how things get done around here. I don't think it's been updated in years."
— Corporate salary administration professional

Heartfelt Leader

Inclusive organizations often request assistance in reviewing the implementation of current HR procedures. Following through on one such consultation, an executive telephoned to extend his gratitude and indicated that he had performed an in-depth analysis of compensation. Though no documents had been shared and only procedural issues discussed, he had a resultant "aha moment" that generated an internal compensation review. That review identified almost two dozen women in mid-level management whose salaries were unjustifiably below those of their peers, thus warranting adjustments. *Many have the conviction but need guidance and support.*

Rules. Regulations. Reality.

Each year employers spend millions of dollars retooling, refining and re-engineering internal HR management policies and procedures. This year the focus might be on retraining, while five years ago the push might have been on encouraging advanced education. In many workplaces the stovepipe hierarchy and upward chain of command have been replaced by matrix management in which one's superior can be in a different location or state or even outside the continental United States. Many procedural changes each year are disseminated via written policies and guidance, while others are found only in an executive's remarks to a board of directors or special interest group.

Communications, consistent, frequent, and varied in format, are one way in which the HR specialist can recalibrate with the C-suite. Therefore, formal written policies and procedures must be reflective of the current goals pursued by the executive management team. Policies and procedures must embody the corporate culture. Practices or organizational designs that arise from outside the company or industry may have cultural disconnects or design flaws that prevent the mirroring of employer successes of other entities. The best "what works" found elsewhere can falter for many reasons. It must be understood that hollow, impractical, or otherwise unwieldy policies simply will not achieve the results desired.

Policies vs. Practices

"A vision that is incapable of evoking action through behavioral change must be regarded as dead!"[1]

One of the ways a CEO affects change is to put a set of policies into play that reinforce the articulated goals. Many chief executives are committed to nondiscrimination and diversity — though many have differing views on what the latter entails. But while they are sincere in their commitment, even communicating that commitment to senior management, mid-management, and the line, it is the practices that are in play that buttress or undercut that commitment. It's not the policies, but the practices that destabilize the success of the efforts and initiatives underway.

As consultants looking in we are given a courtside seat and can review all the practices up close. But, rest assured, employees can see them from their seats — maybe not the full totality of the practices, but disconnects here and there. Human Resources has a front row seat as well, and usually questions the exceptions, especially the most egregious ones. At some point the totality of the exceptions to the rules becomes so great that the rules become meaningless. It is at that point that the C-suite loses credibility, and the sincerity of the commitment is damaged (see Figure 7.1).

Figure 7.1

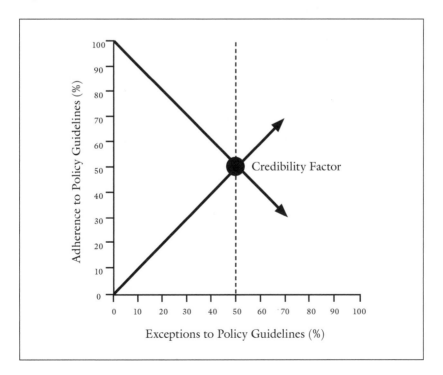

There is no one, singular human resource aspect that is more susceptible to this disconnect than the next. In almost every area of the workplace, we have seen gaps between the well-written, often-articulated policies and the actual practices in play. This can be readily observed in the recruitment and hiring processes at many large employers.

Hiring

Most employers are aware that they have a requirement to ensure nondiscrimination in all aspects of hiring, but others believe having the EEO tagline is the extent of their responsibilities. Large employers have staff members whose sole responsibilities are to recruit or staff positions. These individuals know that they must keep records on: who applies, the point(s) at which some applicants fall out of the process, and the justification for the final selection decision itself.

But while HR manuals describe recruitment and hiring policies in great detail, it is not uncommon to find hires outside the formal HR application process. In these instances, Human Resources is not fully utilized as a valuable, expert resource in staffing, compensation discussions, onboarding support, and administrative needs required. When there is a disconnect between hiring practices and the formal policies, the practices in question often do not result in applicant diversity. The *ganas*-driven managers will work to ensure that disconnects and inconsistencies are minimized. Some specific examples follow.

Hiring Fairs

While recruiters go out to a variety of college and university campuses to recruit, there is much latitude in these processes. Some recruiters only recruit from campuses that, while they are prestigious, do not have a very large, diverse student body. Other recruiters distribute applications on-campus to a subset of those handing in resumes. Some will even take the next step and interview some of those "applicants" while on-campus. Those that "interview well" are moved to the applicant pool, while all others are screened out.

A Case in Point

"Do we have a policy regarding all applicants having to come in through the website or don't we? Every time I turn around there's another person being onboarded who never actually applied." — Staffing director

---

Random Resumes

There is virtually no stopping the random resume. These resumes surface in almost every workplace and have a variety of entry points. They might surface from an applicant pool, from another job vacancy, from a professional colleague, or from a recruiter. While there is nothing inherently wrong with these entries, if the majority of these sources of candidates do not yield diversity, then the HR professional could work with the manager to develop a more balanced pool of applicants. This is especially true in industries that are nontraditional fields for women.

Attitudinal Bias in Hiring

"This case should remind employers that just because discrimination may have been tolerated in a particular industry in the past does not make it right. Federal law requires employers to base hiring on one's qualifications and ability to do the job — not on whether the person is a man or a woman."[2]

Even with strong, straightforward policies in place, the element of personal bias can undermine the diversity efforts. Take the recent lawsuit against a taconite mining operation, which involved a person with a disability. A hearing-impaired applicant was not considered suitable due to his disability — even though he had performed the job for another company satisfactorily. "There is no reason to think that he would be any less successful at [the hiring company] in those positions than he was in his former jobs, where his performance was praised and commended."[3]

Performance Management

"All employees have a right to be judged by their work performance and not their race. This consent decree will help make sure that what happened to [a victim of discrimination] does not happen to any other ... employee."[4]

Regardless of the formal performance management system, the authors' experiences indicate that there is considerable leeway in these systems. Whether the performance management system is narrative-based, a singular rating, multiple ratings, or even ranking of employees, managers find ways to leverage the system in support of their views, often because there is very little oversight of the process. As performance management is a driver in promotions, compensation, and even when downsizing or rightsizing, it is important that performance management practices be reviewed to eradicate any form of bias or prejudice that exists.

Narrative Assessments

All-too-often narrative assessments contain subjective items such as employee looks, religious customs and social networks. Or, the employee receives a perfunctory evaluation devoid of any meaningful feedback, followed by a performance rating or ranking. When narrative assessments bear no correlation to ratings or rankings, credibility is compromised. Narrative assessments alone also give management much discretion in deciding who gets promoted. The "always the bridesmaid never the bride" syndrome can result from a lack of accountability, oversight, and *ganas* for fairness.

Ratings and Rankings

It is common for managers to utilize the ratings or ranking system(s) outside the formal HR guidelines. Some examples include:

» Rating a new employee in order for him/her to receive additional compensation, even when the policy calls for them to be categorized as "too new to rate";

» Rating employees outside the standard annual cycle, to position them for additional opportunities and/or provide additional compensation;

» Rating employees on the low end while their narratives are exemplary.

Performance systems should be spot-checked for completeness, adherence to guidelines, and administration of resulting rewards, as there will always be managers who find "play" in any HR system. Without such, there can be no assurances of fairness and accuracy in performance management administration.

Staffing and Talent Development

Most employers post vacancies and encourage interested employees to apply. Such posting policies create the appearance of openness and inclusiveness and aim to reach out to all sources of talent. Though there are a few employers who post every job up to and including the C-suite, the majority of job posting systems end at the upper mid-levels, just before entry into the senior executive ranks. At this point, the executive staffing and development function takes over. Throughout the years, these high-level senior management positions have been the most difficult and challenging to integrate with diverse talent for a variety of reasons. With just a handful of prospective candidates who can operate at this level, the selection process becomes quite subjective. In addition, there is a tendency to play it safe and not make selection decisions that could be considered risky for the organization. There is also the comfort level that comes with the intimacy of the few leading the many. Long days and nights filled with consecutive meetings make it tempting to involve individuals with whom one feels relaxed and comfortable. Oftentimes, these are individuals who share common characteristics. Leadership profile evaluations and the battery of aptitude tests that are often administered at these levels are customized to reflect the culture and values of the organization. Validation of such tests to ensure they are free of bias might be nonexistent. To make the integration challenge even more difficult, diverse and talented individuals about to reach those levels could decide to leave to start a business or could get recruited away for immediate access into those ranks at another organization.

Given the urgency and sensitivity of these appointments, the tendency to pre-select individuals could become an issue if it violates formal policy. Women report having been told, "feel free to apply, but there's a candidate already identified." Or word gets out through the informal network that "the job is wired; don't bother applying." Additionally, job descriptions can be written person-specific to ensure that the inside track candidate has the "best fit." These practices undercut the efforts of the *ganas*-driven manager to make diversity progress at those levels.

Inconsistencies we have observed include the advancement, promotion, and positioning of individuals who do not have the requisite skills or track record of performance expected. Reviews of placement actions have found incidents where those listed on the succession slate as "ready now" have been passed over for others returning from global assignments, or needing a "holding place," or they have been just plainly bumped out of position by someone else. While this may be nondiscriminatory, if such movements consistently affect women and diverse professionals, it may be that the succession slate and formal processes are not a legitimate component of corporate culture.

One of the most egregious examples of deceptive practices was the EEOC case against a popular steakhouse chain in 2001. A female site director, responsible for acquiring and developing 100 new restaurants a year, was asked to train a new male hire in all of the aspects of her job. Subsequently, the restaurant chain allegedly not only removed almost all of the director's job duties and gave them to the new hire, but also demoted her to a clerical position when she complained. The steakhouse chain also paid the new hire almost twice her salary. "The jury's decision and award in this case reaffirm the principle that gender-based pay discrimination and unlawful retaliation in the workplace cannot be tolerated. I urge all employers to take proactive steps to evaluate their employment policies and practices and to eliminate any and all barriers in the workplace that deprive women of the freedom to compete in the workplace and to achieve their fullest potential."[5]

Compensation

The exceptions to the rule in compensation are innumerable. Compensation systems, by design, allow the manager to differentiate amongst peers in remuneration. The problem is that such differentiation can result in discrimination if the practices substantially favor one group over another without valid justification. While the policies are written to be nondiscriminatory, it is the practices that have gotten many employers in legal trouble. As mentioned in Chapter 6, base pay, which serves as the foundation for a total compensation program that can include bonuses and long-term incentives, should be routinely reviewed to ensure that there are no inherent systemic problems of disparate treatment.

While, in many settings, formal guidelines exist for compensation by level, title, code, band, or range, compensation policies in practice allow for "exceptions to the rule." In general terms these exceptions warrant additional explanation to Human Resources. A review of all exceptions to the rules can often serve as a road map of those who are high potentials, high performers, and "corporate property." This applies to all forms of remuneration: those who get bonuses below the "bonus eligible" level, those who receive stock options outside of guidelines, and those who receive stock grants outside guidelines, etc. The list is extensive. The motivated manager will want all such exceptions monitored to avoid a *Ledbetter* scenario (see Chapter 6).

Terminations

Company-initiated terminations for cause are often classified as "voluntary terminations," which makes it difficult to accurately count the number of people who are terminated involuntarily. Terminations denoted as involuntary are carefully audited internally to ensure actions taken are valid under the law and supportable by documentation. It is in these cases that the general counsel's office may screen performance appraisals and documentation to ensure that there is sufficient cause. A frequent practice is to obtain a signed severance agreement from those who have been terminated involuntarily. In exchange for the signed agreement requiring that the terms be kept confidential and usually involving some financial transaction, the company agrees to treat the separation as "voluntary" and not to disparage the individual before other prospective employers, among other things.

Careful Implementation of New Policies

Countless hours are spent each year by businesses adopting costly programs and initiatives that worked well ... somewhere else. Companies are intent on identifying what competitors are doing and replicating their actions. While, occasionally, another employer's concept or initiative could find fertile ground in your organization, adopting another's practices lock, stock, and barrel is a recipe for disappointment, if not failure. The laundry list of policies that have worked in one situation but not the next is extensive — from formal assigned mentoring programs to pay for performance programs, affinity groups, and work-life balance initiatives. There is no cookie-cutter formula for success, but, rather, each employer must define the mission-connected values that drive employees and translate them into policies and practices that are their own.

Diversity Policies — Separate but Equal?

A school of thought advocated by some diversity specialists and consulting experts involves the creation of programs and policies earmarked exclusively for racial/ethnic minority groups. Instead of just ensuring that the net is wide enough to bring in diversity in hiring, some diversity specialists favor setting aggressive hiring and promotional goals. When these goals become rigid and inflexible, the company becomes vulnerable to criticisms of running a quotas-driven program and could face a backlash from other employees who believe their opportunities to compete are reduced by such practice. Similarly, some diversity specialists proffer the need for separate systems, such as high-potential lists for people of color and women, to ensure they receive the attention of the C-suite. By running these programs on parallel tracks, there is always the real concern that those on the separate list, on the separate path, or in separate training will have fewer opportunities to compete overall.

The other consideration is the stigma that can result from programs that are gender- or race-specific. Wouldn't people of color or women like to know where they stand in terms of skills and experience compared to all eligible others on a list, rather than being put on a separate list that may or may not offer a realistic calibration of their talent? Even if they're near the bottom due to time in title or seniority? Caution is recommended when undertaking separate systems for the identification, development, and promotion of people of color, ethnic minorities, and women. Separate tracking systems might function well at the lower organizational levels when the focus is on attracting diverse talent. It is there that these separate lists could force the questions "where are they?" and "what's it going to take?"

Employers are encouraged to get close to their policies and the actual practices on a routine basis. At a minimum, the disconnect might be eye-opening. For those employers identifying practices undercutting inclusion and diversity, greater oversight is warranted.

Policy Refinement

There should be no hesitancy in withdrawing policies that are simply not working or producing the desired results. There should always be an exit strategy available to counter the volumes of procedures and policies sitting on shelves of well-meaning managers who have failed to implement them due to lack of time, energy, interest, or accountability. History has shown that well-meaning employers, guilty of hanging on to a failed policy or practice, can cause detrimental institutional harm to the company. Have an exit strategy and don't be afraid to use it.

Organizations are moving quickly, making it hard for HR professionals to keep up. Budgets get tighter, and all departments are required to do more with less. Updating formal HR guidance might lag behind all the other competing priorities. The downside is that policies still listed on the books are no longer practiced, or worse, are at odds with current procedures, leading to legal implications. It is recommended that policies be reviewed and updated on a timely basis as a proactive risk-management measure. With more and more companies posting their HR policies on their internal website, technology can enable this effort far more readily than in the old days of page replacements in handbooks.

> "When you have solid, fair employment policies and procedures in place, and you follow them consistently, you are not only being a good employer, you are also protecting yourself from serious liability."[6]

The Truth About Policies

While there are many who chide the issuance of policies and callously state that they'll be obsolete by the time the ink dries, the truth is that sound policies help both the employer and the employee. They add consistency and integrity. They provide a framework by which all can reconnect and be held accountable. Policies work best when the 3 P's are met:

- » Public.
- » Participative.
- » Practical.

Policies that are public in nature and are transparent lead to greater understanding and accountability. Those formulated through the active participation of *all* affected employees lead to greater buy-in and acceptance. Those policies that are practical will ensure that the system closely models the policy.

While there is always discretion in employment policies, when that discretion and the resultant "exceptions" to the rule begin to outnumber the actual policies, it may appear that there is not a system operating at all. When that point is reached, the employment policy may be called into question, and the results found to be subjective, biased, and perhaps even discriminatory.

08 An Appeal to the Heart

"Through our great good fortune, in our youth our hearts were touched with fire. It was given to us to learn at the outset that life is a profound and passionate thing." — Oliver Wendell Holmes[1]

Tête à Tête. Vis á Vis. Mano a Mano. Heart to Heart.

Intelligence, creativity, hard work, drive, honesty, integrity, and empathy for the employee coupled with a strong sense of fairness while embracing diversity and fostering inclusion. Sounds like a straightforward business plan and something to which all could agree — in principle. However, due to competing demands on our time and energies, attitudinal biases, past histories with employees, and the need to produce more with fewer resources, we fall short at times. When we do, it is what we do next that matters most. Much like the baseball phrase "pick me up," which is used between players when one fails by striking out or making an error, there will be plenty of employees (rank-and-file and management alike) there to pick up the *ganas*-driven employer when the going gets tough.

> ### A Case in Point
>
> "All the data I've seen in 30 years of being in business
> — and all of my personal experience at P&G over the last
> 23 years — convince me that a diverse organization will
> out-think, out-innovate, and out-perform a homogenous
> organization every single time. In the end, the buck stops
> with me." — A.G. Lafley, chairman of the board and former
> president and CEO, Procter & Gamble

In the previous chapters, we have discussed most major employment considerations important to the creation of an inclusive, diverse, and just workplace. Throughout these pages, we have described processes, identified issues, illustrated points, and offered ideas for going beyond the ordinary limits of the law to a higher, more rewarding level of achievement. Having done all that, we end this book right where we started, with an appeal to your heart.

It is worth repeating that leadership from the heart requires more than competence; it requires character and confidence. The great humanist psychologist Carl Rogers observed that, "Clarifying your values is the essential step toward a richer, fuller and more productive life."[2] He counseled us to ask ourselves questions such as:

» What do I believe in?
» What puts meaning in my life?
» What qualities are important for my life to be complete?

Anne Mulcahy began her career at Xerox over thirty years ago and just recently stepped down as the company's chairman and CEO. She is credited with saving the company from bankruptcy and restoring its luster. Mulcahy embodies the values and promotes the proud heritage of a company that invested heavily in attracting, developing, and retaining diverse talent, long before others recognized the business advantages for doing so. Back in the 1970s and 1980s, Xerox was a benchmark company, setting the standard for the development of people of color and women, particularly in line positions. Former Xerox CEO David Kearns is legendary in business and industry circles for his passion, his *ganas*, toward advocating and actively championing the development of professionals of color and women. Xerox became the company to *recruit from* when other companies were looking for high quality, diverse talent. Consequently, many black executives, trained and developed at Xerox, became role models for and proponents of inclusive, diversity-focused development efforts once recruited to other companies. Some say that over time, leadership changes and other business pressures diverted Xerox's attention away from its earlier attention to diversity, until Mulcahy took over.

Having been a product of that earlier culture, Mulcahy went back to the company's roots to lead it. When asked how an organization makes sure that women, people of color, and others not historically found in the management suites are included, she answered, "Our commitment begins at the top, with total executive commitment."[3] By leading from the top, the CEO empowers others to follow suit. HR professionals and line managers desiring to lead with their hearts become emboldened in their efforts when their top executive sets the tone and direction.

As part of her earlier professional development, Mulcahy rotated through the HR function, serving as vice president of HR at Xerox. Of that experience, she says, "Leading the human resources team at Xerox was one of the most valuable jobs of my career."[4] Like Anne Mulcahy, and David Kearns before her, the person at the top must have the commitment, the vision, and the *ganas*, to exercise leadership in this area. But they can't do it alone. They need people at every level of the organization to take ownership of the process.

Empowerment with Accountability

People at the local level must be given the responsibility to lead, along with the tools necessary to exercise effective leadership, and also be held accountable for the results. Accountability ensures that no one can take a pass; no one can rely on the efforts of others. Conversely, even when the C-suite is distracted from driving diversity and inclusion efforts (or unfortunately simply disinterested), each and every person working for fairness can sustain them. For it is the totality of each and every HR decision that makes a good company. It is through the empowerment of the employee that a sense of ownership will result. It is amazing to see the transformation an empowered manager can make — from including others in meetings to proactively soliciting the views of all, from providing face time with executives in a large group to having others present, from dodging employee problems to problem-solving with employees, and from self-promotion to promoting high-performing talent up and out.

"By empowering others to follow your footsteps, you not only prepare them for success but also position yourself as a leader on a path toward greater responsibility."[5]

HR professionals can help guide the process from the transactional to the transformational by recognizing that, to be effective, they must work with the C-suite and the line managers from their point of reference, from where "their heads are at," enabling them to first promote compliance with the laws, then commitment to the principles embodied in the laws, and ultimately empowering them to reach and sustain beliefs and ideals that transcend the rigidity of the laws. Not everyone reaches this level of high-order thinking at the same time. Some may never get to that level. But it is up to the HR professional to guide the process and enlighten the way through steps designed to build character and grow confidence while yielding results. Every decision, every action that avoids liability while enhancing productivity and employee satisfaction makes it easier to rely more on one's values and less on structured, legal requirements.

Heartfelt Appreciation

Confidence comes from seeing results, from being valued and appreciated for contributions made, and from knowing ourselves and respecting our own individuality. Heartfelt leaders understand that injustice is never about numbers — it is about individuals. It is about the face-to-face conversations on performance, organizational needs, growth areas, and even those times when disciplinary actions are needed. Success will come to enlightened individuals working together with enlightened organizations: organizations that will maintain and support a culture of creativity, ingenuity, and professional growth, and individuals who will be allowed to contribute to their fullest potential, regardless of their race, color, gender, or any other irrelevant personal characteristic.

> "For many, a culture of appreciation that reinforces the company's stated values is the best strategy to achieve the company's mission. A culture of appreciation allows for an individualistic approach to accomplish tasks, but unites employees across geographic and divisional boundaries through a common attitude of recognition for tasks well-done and goals achieved."[6]

We've Come a Long Way … But, the Best Is Yet to Come

When Congress passed the Civil Rights Act of 1964, over 40 years ago, we were embarking on a journey into uncharted territory. No one was sure where we would end up on that journey. Today, our standards as a society are higher and our tolerance for discrimination much lower. For the generations just entering the workplace, it is difficult to fathom a time when it was not illegal to deny someone a job or a promotion because of race or gender. As the demographics of our workforce continue to shift in profound ways, so do the boundaries of the issues we face. The journey begun by the passage of the Civil Rights Act is a continuum, bridging lessons from the past. As fellow passengers on this journey, we must honor the progress we have made and stay on course to ensure full access and inclusion of all who call America home. Staying on course will depend on the spirit and strength of the values that unite us and on our determination to foster workplaces that are open and inclusive of everyone. And real progress will come from the influence each one of us has to drive change and make a difference, one action at a time, one person at a time:

» By having integrity in all actions;

» By being honest and empathetic simultaneously;

» By reaching out and going beyond traditional practices;

» By championing the advancement of those deserving of opportunities and recognition; and

» By leading by example, with actions not just words.

Indeed, our motivation, our *ganas*, is the key to our success as individuals and as a nation. Working together, we can unleash the creativity and productivity of *all of our workers*. After all, we are connected — business-to-business, citizen-to-citizen, and neighbor-to-neighbor. May these pages touch your heart with fire, and may you live your day today the way you would always want to be remembered by those whose lives you'll touch.

Endnotes

Preface

1. "Sandra Day O'Connor: First Woman Justice of the Supreme Court." April 27, 2008. Available at: http://www.america.gov/st/diversity-english/2008/April/20080427123230eaifas0.6004755.html.

2. Linda Greenhouse, "The Supreme Court: Affirmative Action; Justices Back Affirmative Action by 5 to 4, But Wider Vote Bans a Racial Point System," *The New York Times*, June 24, 2003. Available at: http://www.nytimes.com/2003/06/24/us/supremecourt-affirmative-action-justices-back-affirmative-action-5-4-butwider.html. *Grutter v. Bollinger*, 539 U.S. 306 (2003) is available at www.law.cornlee.edu/supct/html/02-241.ZS.html.

Chapter 1

1. "The Life of Thurgood Marshall Celebrated at Washington National Cathedral," The Archives of the Episcopal Church. Episcopal Press and News. 93020. February 2, 1993.

2. W. Edwards Deming, *The New Economics* (Cambridge: Massachusetts Institute of Technology. 1994). p. 52.

3. News & Notes. *Workspan*. March 2007, 9.

4. "New College Graduates Seeking Employers with Integrity," National Association of Colleges and Employers Graduating Student and Alumni Survey. Smartpro.com.

5. The Credo. www.jnj.com.

6. Authors' personal files.

7. "Majority of American workers agree: more diverse workforce equals more successful organization," Adecco. Melville, New York, July 10, 2008. Available at: www.adeccousa.com/AboutUs/Pages/NewsContent.aspx?.

8. Transcript of remarks from Freedom to Compete Ceremony. 2005.

9. "Employee Discrimination in the Workplace," The Gallup Organization. December 8, 2005. Available at http://media.gallup.com/government/PDF/Gallup_Discrimination_Report_Final.pdf.

Chapter 2

1. Lance Secretan, "Pioneer in Leadership Theory," *Industry Week*, October 12, 1998.

2. Harold L. Lee, "The Defining Decade: Kettering Medical Center Network," 2005. 58.

3. "Bridges Spotlight," *AHA News*, vol. 40. no. 4. February 23, 2004.

4. Authors' personal files.

5. Ibid.

6. Statement by Mark Nagel, authors' personal files.

7. "WOLF Meets Business." Available at: www.wolfinspires.com.

8. "Women Leading Change — Julie Gilbert, Leader of the WOLF Pack at Best Buy," Available at: www.eurpeanpwn.net/index.php?article_id=622.

Chapter 3

1. Anne Morrow Lindbergh, *Gift from the Sea* (New York. Pantheon Books, 1955), 38, 50.

2. Sara Vallas, "Communication is Key to Total Rewards Success," *Workspan*, October 2006, 25-26.

3. "Lawmakers Paralyzed by Twitter during Obama Speech," *The Washington Post*, February 25, 2009. Available at: http://www.huffingtonpost.com/2009/02/25/lawmakers-paralyzed-by-tw_n_169774.html.

4. Rene Henry, direct communications with author. Correspondence on file.

5. Barbara Levin, "How Technology Changed Hershey's Culture of Employee Communications," *Workspan*, April 2008, 66.

6. Careerbuilder.com. Available at: http://www.careerbuilder.com/ Jobs/Company/C388V70KXZNXCKTXMW/Ryder-Logistics-T ransportation/?cbsid=b5d480b0eec24d3b82f85ecf97d13514- 291658526-wj-6&&ns_siteid=ns_us_g_Internet_Week_%20_ ryd_&cbRecursionCnt=1.

7. http://www.ryder.com/aboutus_diversity_letter.html.

8. Nigel Paine, "Talent Will Out," *Talent Management Magazine*, February 2007, 16.

9. "Online Extra: The Six Ps of PepsiCo's Chief," *BusinessWeek*, January 10, 2005. Available at: www.businessweek.com/print/maga- zine/content/05_02/b3915637.htm.

10. Ibid.

11. David Creelman and Norm Smallwood, "Reporting to Wall Street About Diversity." WITI Women. Available at: http://www.witi. com/women/2005/diversity.php.

12. Jennifer Millman, "Women Shareholders: Are you using your proxy power?" Diversityinc.com. January 17, 2008.

13. Alan Mulally, "Ford Motor Company: A Word About Diversity and Inclusion from our CEO." Available at: www.ford.com/our- values/diversity/diversity-ford/diversity-inclusion-ceo/mulally.

14. Op. cit. "Online Extra."

15. Yoji Cole, "5 Ways to Get Middle Managers to Push Diversity." See www.diversityinc.com.

16. Noelle C. Nelson, "Good Grievances: While it's easier to revel in the praise, listening and responding to employee gripes shows your mettle as a manager," *HR Magazine*, October 2006. 114.

Chapter 4

1. Tony Dungy, "Uncommon: Finding Your Path to Significance," *The New York Times*, February 20, 2009.

2. Jeff Benrey, "Silicon Valley: Viewpoint: Fishing for Talent with Sharks in the Water," *Workspan*, June 2008, 74.

3. Stan LaPeak and Lowell Williams. Survey by *Workforce Management* and EquaTerra Global. December, 2008.

4. *Antoine de Saint-Exupery* (1900-1944).

5. Diversity Briefs. Women in Business & Industry. 15.

6. Khanyi Nkosi, "Boardroom Challenges that Can Make Success Difficult," *Sowetan*, May 7, 2009. Available at: http://www.sowetan.co.za/News/Business/Article.aspx?id=993950.

7. Personal conversation with author.

8. "The Employer's Guide to College Recruiting and Hiring," National Association of Colleges and Employers, 2007, See www.naceweb.org/products/info_pages/empguide.htm.

9. "On Campus Recruiting," *The Emerging Professional*, July 13, 2009. Available at: http://emergingprofessional.typepad.com/the_emerging_professional/oncampus_recruiting.

10. "Overview of Structural Barriers." SAA Literature: Ethnic Entrepreneurship. See http://alumni.eecs.berkeley.edu/.

11. Kids Count Indicator Brief: Reducing the High School Drop Out Rate. Annie E. Casey Foundation. July 2003, 4.

12. Bill Roberts, "Manage Candidates Right from the Start," *HR Magazine*, October 2008. 76.

13. Office of Federal Contract Compliance Programs, U.S. Department of Labor. See http://www.dol.gov/esa/ofccp/regs/compliance/faqs/iappfaqs.htm#Q1GI.

14. Jennifer Taylor Arnold, "Employee Referrals at a Keystroke," *HR Magazine*, October 2006, 84.

15. "50 Best Small & Medium Companies to Work for in America," *HR Magazine*, July 2008, 51.

16. Ibid. 86.

17. "Sign of the Times: Temp-to-Perm Attorneys," *HR Magazine*, January 2009, 24.

18. Authors' personal files.

19. Ibid.

20. Ibid.

21. Op. cit. Benrey, Jeff. 74.
22. *EEOC v. Abercrombie & Fitch Stores, Inc.*, No. 04-4731 (N.D. Cal. April 14, 2005). See www.eeoc.gov/litigation/settlements.
23. OFCCP Blogspot. See http://ofccp.blogspot.com/2007/10/recent-ofccp-settlements.html.
24. "Final Decree Entered with Walgreens for $24 Million in Landmark Race Discrimination Suit by EEOC: Class of More Than 10,000 to Receive Monetary Relief; Significant Injunctive Remedies Included." EEOC press release. See http://www.eeoc.gov/press/3-25-08.html.
25. *EEOC v. Victor-Arch Inc.* See http://www.wageproject.org/sexdiscDB/sexdiscDB.php?mode=full&id=454.
26. Employment Agency to Pay $250,000 for Job Discrimination, Retaliation. July 11, 2009. See http://ohsonline.com/Articles/2009/07/11/Employment-Agency-to-Pay-250000.aspx.
27. "In Indianapolis, Renhill Staffing To Pay $580,000 To Settle EEOC Age, Race and Retaliation Suit." Equal Employment Opportunity Commission. June 29, 2008. See http://www.employmentlawfirms.com/regional-content.cfm/state/in/Article/116791/In-Indianapolis-Renhill-Staffing-To.html.

Chapter 5

1. "No Limits on Opportunity. Meet Karen King, President, East Division," McDonald's. See www.aboutmcdonalds.com.
2. Personal conversation with author.
3. The HR Café: The Business Case for Onboarding. Available at: http://hrcafe.typepad.com/my_weblog/2009/02/the-business-case-for-onboarding.html.
4. Brian D. Lowenthal, "The Five Stages of New Hire Orientation and Onboarding," The Benchmark Partners, LLC. Available at: http://media.monster.com/a/i/intelligence/pdf/OnBoarding_111606_Webinar.pdf.

5. Donald N. Bersoff, "Should Subjective Employment Devices be Scrutinized? It's Elementary, My Dear Ms. Watson," *American Psychologist*, vol. 43(12), 1988, 1016-18.

6. Nancy Noelke, "Leverage the Present to Build the Future," *HR Magazine*, March 2009, 35-6.

7. Linda K. Stroh, Jeanne M. Brett, and Anne H. Reilly, "All the Right Stuff: A Comparison of Female and Male Managers' Career Progression," *Journal of Applied Psychology*, October 22, 1991.

8. Robert J. Thomas, "Life's Hard Lessons." *HR Magazine*, June 2008, 143.

9. "A Report on the Glass Ceiling Initiative," U.S. Department of Labor. 1990.

10. "Global Relocation Trends Show Future Expat Growth," A 2008 Survey by GMAS Global Relocation Services. Available at: http://www.goinglobal.com/newsletter/march09corp_general_global.asp.

11. Author conversation with IBM executives.

12. "New Catalyst Study Reveals Financial Performance is Higher for Companies with More Women at the Top," See http://www.catalystwomen.org/.

Chapter 6

1. Online Exclusive: "Diversity and Inclusion: The Big Picture." *Progressive Grocer*. August 1, 2008. Available at: http://www.progressivegrocer.com/progressivegrocer/content_display/features/corporate-social-responsibility/e3i1e5a2e8d39dee108fb86d3ef7e5d0f42?imw=Y.

2. "Giving Performance Appraisals." Hays Consulting. See www.hays.ca/employers/giving-performance-appraisals.aspx.

3. Hudson Highland Group. *Pay and Performance in America: 2005 Compensation and Benefits Report*. 2005. See http://ca.hudson.com/documents/us-papers-pay-performance.pdf.

4. Shankar Vedaneam, "Study Ties Wage Disparities To Outlook on Gender Roles," *The Washington Post*, September 22, 2008.

Available at: http://www.washingtonpost.com/wp-dyn/content/article/2008/09/21/AR2008092102529.html.

5. Fred Nickol, "Don't Redesign Your Company's Performance Appraisal System. Scrap it," 2000. See http://home.att.net/-nickols/scrap_it.htm.

6. Jacqueline Landau, "The Relationship of Race and Gender to Managers' Ratings of Promotion Potential," *Journal of Organizational Behavior*, volume 16, no. 4. July 1995. 391-400.

7. Op. cit. Vallas, Sara. 25-26.

8. Susan Gunelius, "Women Make 77 Cents for Each Dollar Men Make in the U.S.," See http://www.womenonbusiness.com/women-make-77-cents-for-each-dollar-men-make-in-the-us.

9. Evelyn Murphy with E.J. Graff, *Getting Even: Why Women Don't Get Paid Like Men — and What to Do About It* (New York: Simon and Schuster, 2005) 226.

10. *Ledbetter v. Goodyear Tire & Rubber Co., Inc.*, 550 U. S. 618 (2007).

11. Susan M. Heathfield, "360 Degree Feedback: The Good, the Bad, and the Ugly." See http://humanresources.about.com/library/weekly/aa042501a.htm.

12. Larry (blogger), HR Morning. In response to: Giuliano, Jim. "Should you self-audit to protect against 'Ledbetter' complaints." See http://www.hrmorning.com/should-you-self-audit-to-protect-against-ledbetter-complaints/.

13. "EEOC Sues Sterling for Discrimination." EEOC press release. September 25, 2008.

14. Gary MacHR (blogger), HR Morning. In response to: Giuliano, Jim. "Should you self-audit to protect against 'Ledbetter' complaints." See http://www.hrmorning.com/should-you-self-audit-to-protect-against-ledbetter-complaints/.

15. Op. cit. The Gallup Organization. 8.

16. Ibid.

Chapter 7

1. Amanor-Boadu, Agricultural Marketing Resource Center. See www.agmrc.org/agmrc/business/startingbusiness/strategicoverview.html.

2. "Union Pacific to Pay $75,000 for Sex Bias and Implement Policy Changes to Settle Suit: Federal Agency Claimed Railroad Refused to Hire Female Foreman," EEOC press release. Available at: http://www.eeoc.gov/press/2-3-09.html. February 3, 2009.

3. "Hibbing Taconite Company Sued by EEOC for Disability Discrimination." EEOC press release. March 31, 2009.

4. "J.C. Penney to Pay $50,000 to Settle EEOC Race Discrimination Suit." EEOC press release. February 12, 2009.

5. "Jury Finds Outback Steakhouse Guilty of Sex Discrimination and Illegal Retaliation; Awards Victim $2.2 Million." EEOC press release. September 19, 2001.

6. Management's self-inflicted problems. 1999. Guided Learning Systems LLC. See www.guidedlearning.com/awd/problems-30.html.

Chapter 8

1. Oliver Wendell Holmes Jr., address before John Sedgwick Post No. 4, Grand Army of the Republic, Keene, New Hampshire, May 30, 1884.

2. "Whose Life Is It Anyway?" See http://www.usu.edu/arc/idea_sheets/pdf/whose_life_is_it.pdf

3. "How diversity breeds business results," See www.xerox.com/diversity.

4. Scott Beagrie, "The Magnificent Seven," *Personnel Today*, January 13, 2004. Available at: http://www.personneltoday.com/articles/2004/01/13/21868/the-magnificent-seven.html.

5. Helene Lollis, "Be a Steppingstone. Managers who show employees the path to the top — and help them get there — advance their own careers," *HR Magazine*, November 2008. 112.

6. Derek Irvine, "Designing Your Company's Social Architecture to Engage Employees," Globoforce. *Workspan*, September 2008. 78.

Index

About the Authors

Cari M. Dominguez is the owner of Dominguez & Associates, a management consulting firm that provides selective services in the areas of workforce assessments and diversity evaluations. Dominguez serves on several for profit and nonprofit boards and has numerous professional affiliations. Her public service includes being the former Chair of the Equal Employment Opportunity Commission (EEOC), Director of the Office of Federal Contract Compliance Programs (OFCCP), and Department of Labor's Assistant Secretary for the Employment Standards Administration. In the private sector she was a partner and director at two international executive search firms and held a number of senior human resources positions with Bank of America, where she had responsibility for EEO, succession planning, executive compensation, and talent development.

Judith (Jude) Sotherlund, president of Sotherlund Consulting, is a corporate consultant and published author. Her public service includes serving as Deputy Assistant Secretary of Labor for Employment Standards and as a Staff Assistant in the Office of Communications at The White House. Private-sector experience includes Vice President of Employment Advisory Services Inc., a senior consultant to the Equal Employment Advisory Council (EEAC), and Director of Communications for the National Committee for Quality Health Care.

Additional SHRM-Published Books

The Cultural Fit Factor: Creating an Employment Brand that Attracts, Retains, and Repels the Right Employees
By Lizz Pellet

The Employer's Immigration Compliance Desk Reference
By Gregory H. Siskind

The Essential Guide to Federal Employment Laws
By Lisa Guerin and Amy DelPo

Hiring Source Book
By Catherine D. Fyock

HR and the New Hispanic Workforce: A Comprehensive Guide to Cultivating and Leveraging Employee Success
By Louis E.V. Nevaer and Vaso Perimenis Ekstein

Igniting Gen B & Gen V: The Rules of Engagement for Boomers, Veterans, and Other Long-Terms on the Job
By Nancy S. Ahlrichs

The Legal Context of Staffing
By Jean M. Phillips and Stanley M. Gully

The Manager's Guide to HR: Hiring, Firing, Performance Evaluations, Documentation, Benefits, and Everything Else You Need to Know
By Max Muller

Managing Diversity: A Complete Desk Reference & Planning Guide
By Lee Gardenswartz and Anita Rowe

Reinventing Talent Management: How to Maximize Performance in the New Marketplace
By William A. Schiemann

Rethinking Retention in Good Times and Bad: Breakthrough Ideas for Keeping Your Best Workers
By Richard P. Finnegan

Stop Bullying at Work: Strategies and Tools for HR and Legal Professionals
By Teresa A. Daniel

Strategic Staffing: A Comprehensive System for Effective Workforce Planning
By Thomas P. Bechet

Trainer's Diversity Source Book
By Jonamay Lambert and Selma Myers

For these and other SHRM-published books, please visit
www.shrm.org/publications/books/pages/default.aspx.